D1359118

"This rich and readable volume not only describes so
saints but offers a model for others who could give fle
what the scriptures call 'The Great Cloud of Witnesse

> Lawrence S. Cunningham
> The University of Notre Dame

"In *Project Holiness*, the experience of marriage is narrated by couples who are in
the trenches, striving to respond to the universal call to holiness. Their candid
and often poignant sharing of friendship and sexuality, service and hospitality,
suffering and fidelity will enrich the marriage of those who read this well-
researched and wise book."

> Robert F. Morneau
> Pastor of Resurrection Parish
> Auxiliary Bishop Emeritus of Green Bay

"The Second Vatican Council testified that every Christian, without exception,
is called to holiness of life. In *Project Holiness*, Bridget Burke Ravizza and Julie
Donovan Massey illustrate beautifully how spouses grow in holiness not outside
of their marriage but in the real, often messy, but always abundantly hopeful and
richly graced dynamics of married life. What makes this book special is that it
offers a theology of marriage rooted in the narratives and experiences of married
persons. What makes it a blessing is that it reveals there are saints all around
us, wives and husbands who radiate the love, goodness, compassion, justice, and
joy of God to one another, to their families and faith communities, and to the
world. *Project Holiness* is a gift not only to married couples, but also to those who
minister to them, to church leaders who teach about marriage, and to anyone
preparing for marriage."

> Paul J. Wadell
> Professor of Theology & Religious Studies
> St. Norbert College

"*Project Holiness* honors the experiences and wisdom of married couples and
brings their voices to center of theological reflection on marriage. The result
is a rich and engaging vision of discipleship as it is lived in a 'workshop' of
friendship, fidelity, and forgiveness. *Project Holiness* should be required reading
for bishops and anyone involved in the pastoral care of married couples and
families. It is a model of deep listening that is open to being challenged and
transformed by those everyday saints who are preaching the gospel of the family
in our midst."

> Mary M. Doyle Roche
> Associate Professor, College of the Holy Cross
> Author of *Schools of Solidarity: Families and Catholic Social Teaching*

Project Holiness

Marriage as a Workshop for Everyday Saints

Real Wisdom from Real Married Couples

Bridget Burke Ravizza
Julie Donovan Massey

LITURGICAL PRESS
Collegeville, Minnesota

www.litpress.org

1   2   3   4   5   6   7   8   9

Library of Congress Cataloging-in-Publication Data

Ravizza, Bridget Burke.
   Project holiness : marriage as a workshop for everyday saints : real wisdom
from real married couples / Bridget Burke Ravizza and Julie Donovan Massey.
    pages cm
   Includes bibliographical references.
   ISBN 978-0-8146-3704-3 — ISBN 978-0-8146-3729-6 (ebook)
    1. Marriage—Religious aspects—Christianity. 2. Spouses—Religious life.
   3. Love—Religious aspects—Christianity. I. Ravizza, Bridget Burke. II. Title.
  BV4596.M3M385   2015
  248.8'44—dc23   2014047039

To my mom and dad, Barbara and Tom Burke, whose fidelity to one another is an inspiration and whose joy in one another is a delight.

To my in-laws, Mike and Dodie Ravizza, who first taught John how to love and who have extended their love to include me.

To Anne Marie Mongoven, OP, who encouraged my vocation as theologian and teacher.

To Clare, who makes me laugh and makes me proud.

To John, who had the courage (and, let's face it, good sense) to marry me, which is the greatest blessing of my life.

BBR

To my parents, John and Marcia Donovan, who showed us kids what a devoted and loving partnership looks like and who set the bar high!

To my in-laws, Jack and Colleen Massey, who raised a son who believes family comes first and who expanded the boundaries of their family to me.

To the many teachers who asked me questions that linger, and especially Mary Elsbernd, OSF, who showed me what a scholarly woman of faith looks like.

To my incredible daughters Shannon, Megan, and Bridget, who show me God's face in ways distinct and wonderful; being your mother is a privilege and grace.

To Shawn, who—after we accidentally met in a seminary bar—has been purposefully loving and supporting me and who gives his whole heart to anything he commits to, especially me!

JDM

Contents

Preface

"There are many stories when you're as old as we are," the woman we were interviewing noted. "And that's what I'm sure you are looking for . . . because God teaches through stories. God taught in the Bible through parables and [is] teaching us through our own story."

As researchers, we agreed wholeheartedly with her assertion. Belief in the wisdom to be found in real-life stories motivated us to write a book about Catholic marriage that is grounded in the experience of real couples, highlighting the virtues, values, and practices that make Catholic marriages successful and that foster each spouse's ability to live out the call to holiness. We were aware of insightful, theological works on Catholic marriage, many of which we draw on and feel indebted to, but we wanted to write a book that began in story, and honored lived experience from preface to conclusion. We entered into our research believing in the insight our subjects would possess.

A man in our very first focus group shared our conviction about the power of story: "If I were to write a document on marriage, I would go to the [morning] Mass, and I'd tell the stories I know. I'd talk about [couples in the parish] and in my own life. And you can't tell the story until you've seen all the chapters. I'd tell the story of my parents . . . when you see parents who once fought viciously, and one parent is now [struggling with dementia] and the other is taking care of her with patience that you never saw when you were a kid, you understand what marriage is. And it's in the documents, but the stories make it real."

It is our belief that as we highlight virtues, values, and practices needed for married holiness, the stories of the couples we met will "make it real" for you as reader as they surely did for us. In this preface we will share a bit more of the story of how we came to write this book, introductory notes on our methodology, and a glimpse of what lies ahead.

Hearing from Saints: *You Must Tell the Story!*

Bridget, an associate professor of theology and religious studies, traces the origin of this project to the 2011 meeting of the Catholic Theological Society of America in San Jose, California. During that conference, she attended a panel entitled "Scripting the Saints," composed of authors and theologians who write about the communion of saints.[1] During the question-and-answer period, one of the panelists, Professor Lawrence Cunningham of the University of Notre Dame, said that he has repeatedly suggested to his graduate students that a fascinating project would be to travel around the country in order to talk to "ordinary saints"—men and women who are identified by others in their parish communities as particularly holy. He argued that the church could learn a great deal about holiness and discipleship by hearing these saints tell their stories. Cunningham's point is well-taken; while we often think of saints as supernatural heroes who lived in another place and time, it is also true that many of us readily could point to persons in our own church communities about whom we would say, "Oh, she's a saint!" These ordinary saints are a valuable and largely untapped resource in theological thinking.[2]

Inspired by Cunningham's comment, Bridget knew that she wanted to actively seek out Catholic married couples who are identified as particularly holy, or saintly, by others in their church communities. She was determined to listen to their stories and glean their wisdom about married life and holiness in order to pass that wisdom along to others. And she knew just with whom she wanted to embark on this journey: her friend and colleague, Julie.

Julie, a lay minister who has worked in church and academic settings, also has an interest in Catholic marriage and family life and in thinking about everyday holiness, concerns she dates back to graduate school. At the time Julie was completing her final semester's coursework in an MDiv program at Loyola University Chicago, she and her newly married husband were delighted to learn they were expecting their first child. As the pregnancy progressed, she began to share this exciting news with her circle of friends. Word that Julie was pregnant quickly spread around Loyola's Institute for Pastoral Studies. She became accustomed to fellow students, faculty, and staff sharing a word of congratulations. But Julie was caught off guard when she was stopped one day by a much-respected professor of church history for what appeared an urgent matter. The professor was a married woman, the mother of two children, and an exceptional teacher with a stunning intellect. She first congratulated Julie on the pregnancy and then said, "You must tell the story of how our everyday lives are holy. The only stories that get told in our tradition are of a holiness that is distant from the ways most of us live." Julie's recollection is that in the moment she responded with great eloquence, saying something along the lines of, "Umm . . . okay." But the professor's imploring has stayed with her and continues to whisper like a calling that will not be forgotten.

Though convinced as researchers that ordinary holiness both could and should be explored, we found that this concept was not always easy for our subjects to engage. That we are not often invited to see the holiness present in the messiness of family life is supported by one man who emailed us in response to the invitation for him and his wife to be interviewed for this book: "[My wife] and I think that you sent this request to the wrong mailbox! If you are looking for models of holiness, you might need to try the other couples named. If you want stories of just two ordinary people striving to do the best they can to make marriage work—fairly well on some days, not so well on others—we would be happy to be interviewed."

Happily, they *were* interviewed, and our conversation elicited much more evidence of holiness than they gave themselves credit for. This was a common exchange early in our interviews: one or more persons would laugh, betraying a bit of discomfort, and suggest maybe we had gotten their name by mistake. We would assure them, remind them that their name had come to us from someone in their parish who saw them as exemplars of married holiness, and invite them to see that naming as affirmation and blessing. To help you understand how we got their names, let us share a bit about our research process.

Our Methodology[3]

This study is grounded in a qualitative research process that enabled us to listen deeply to the lived experience of married persons actively engaged in their Catholic parishes. We began by identifying two midwestern dioceses that afforded some diversity of setting and population. Within these dioceses we identified twenty partner parishes, each of which had a staff person (sometimes the pastor, but most often a pastoral associate or parish administrator) who agreed to assist us in this research by connecting us with parish members. Not every parish to which we reached out responded or agreed to help. Without the help of those who did, our research would have come to a screeching halt.

With the partner parishes identified, we developed a survey and asked the parish staff member to distribute it to five couples (ten people) who had been married eight years or more, are active in their parish, and whose marriages appeared to be successful and flourishing. Some staff members approached a sixth couple, so in the end, 210 surveys were distributed, and 168 were returned to us. These surveys provided us with statistical data and commentary, both of which shaped the topics we explored with couples we interviewed. The surveys also asked respondents to share names of couples in their parishes they see as models of holiness. That became the pool of names from which we invited people to meet with us for interviews.

We had the privilege of meeting with fifty couples. To engage these couples, we conducted twenty-four interviews: twelve ninety-minute interviews with a single couple and twelve two-hour-long focus groups made up of no more than four couples. The interviews were recorded and transcribed, and the reader will meet these couples throughout the text. Those we interviewed impressed us with their insight and vulnerability, and the courage they had in not whitewashing their lived experience, but in telling us the truth of their struggles to live out everyday holiness in marriage and family life. To borrow a term from another qualitative researcher, we found our subjects to be nothing short of brilliant, and hope we allow their brilliance to shine through the pages of this text.[4]

While we did not agree with the theological viewpoint of every person we interviewed, we nonetheless respected the variety of experiences and perspectives expressed by the couples. They became our conversation partners as writers, as we trust they will become yours; we envision this text as a conversation partner for anyone who wishes to understand, or attempt to live out, holiness in marriage.

About the Names: *Why Don't You Just Use Our Real Names?*

As might be expected, the subject names contained throughout this text are pseudonyms. Well into the research process, we were meeting with a focus group that included a member with a good deal of writing experience. Before we had the participants sign consent forms, we were going through our usual commentary about not using real names or identifying information when he asked, "Why don't you just use our real names?" We laughed, and Julie said, "Because we have already met with thirty people, and we told all of them we would not use their real names; too late to turn back now!"

In promising anonymity, we attempted to create an interview environment in which couples could speak most freely, without concern of being identified. We also made a deliberate choice not to use composite characters. So the reader will encounter names, lots of names. And if you see a particular name in one chapter and it appears again in a later chapter, it is the same person, the same couple's story. We do not expect the reader to keep all of the couples straight, or to recall exactly what has been said in earlier chapters. If there is a detail you need to know to contextualize a particular comment, we provide it. We chose not to use composite characters in order to honor the depth and distinction of the couples we met, painting as true to real-life pictures of our participants as possible. In doing so, we hope we have offered the full texture of their voices while still protecting their privacy. The subjects you meet in the following pages are not characters. They are real people—only the names are fake!

What Lies Ahead: *A Map for the Reader*

The text is built around six major themes. While there are many significant virtues, values, and practices in play for successful marriages that foster holiness, these six emerged as the central categories that shape the lives of our subjects. In the text, we treat each theme in turn, and then offer some concluding thoughts and information.

Chapter 1 looks at the place of friendship in marriage, exploring what a deep theological understanding of friendship entails and how that understanding is lived out in the context of marriage. Chapter 2 explores topics of sexuality, including consideration of the diverse ways in which marriages are generative as well as explicit consideration of parenting in marriage. Chapter 3 reflects on the place of ritual in marriage and family life and explores an understanding of marriage as sacrament that reveals the presence of God. Chapter 4 examines the ways that Christian marriage moves us to live out of an ethic of hospitality and service. Chapter 5 grapples with the experience of suffering that is inevitable in every marriage and explores the ways couples navigate suffering in light of faith. Chapter 6 attends to the nature of fidelity and how couples frame and honor their understanding of faithful commitment to one another. The conclusion offers our final perspective on what we heard and implications drawn for both married couples and the wider community of the church. Finally, an appendix is included that expounds on our research method; describes the attributes of our survey sample, with some comparative data from wider populations; and provides detailed data from the survey.

It would be artificial to suggest that the various themes of the text exist in a neat or linear way. In lived experience, these themes overlap regularly and sometimes poignantly. We hope it helps you as reader to see the map of what lies ahead, to know that a topic that may receive a light touch in one place is treated more fully in another. May your journey through these pages be an experience of gift and grace as our journey with the couples we met—on paper and in person—surely was!

Acknowledgments

First and foremost, we thank the couples that participated in our research, whose experiences are the heart of this book. Your willingness to honestly share your stories and open your lives to us moved us deeply and filled us with gratitude. Thank you for your trust and for the many moments of laughter, vulnerability, and wisdom that made our conversations with you both joy and gift. We hope this book honors your goodness.

Thank you to the behind-the-scenes heroes, our parish contacts, who distributed written surveys, helped us contact couples, set up meeting spaces for interviews, and warmly welcomed us to your parishes. Your hospitality—that included unlocking buildings on evenings and weekends, tracking down extension cords, and providing coffee and snacks—was remarkable, and your assistance essential. We are indebted.

We are grateful for support (monetary, emotional, spiritual, and intellectual) given by so many at St. Norbert College. Dean Jeff Frick, Vice President Jay Fostner, OPraem, and a summer grant from the Office of Faculty Development helped fund the project. Julie acknowledges with gratitude the college's support in awarding her a staff sabbatical, making space in her schedule for this important work. She also thanks her colleagues in Mission & Ministry for being model ministers and compassionate colleagues who challenge her to faithful service and who make work a joyful place to be. Bridget thanks the members of the Theology and Religious Studies Discipline for being brilliant teacher-scholars who push her to be better and keep her laughing. TRS colleagues, you are simply the best.

Breanna Mekuly, our trusted transcriber: your help was indispensable, your enthusiasm priceless ("This one's a gold mine!"). Paul Schnorr, thank you for sound advice on all things sociological. We now have data to show that conversations about Likert scales can be both informative and fun if they take place at Titletown Brewery. Luna Café, you are the book's "home office"; thanks for letting us linger for hours—when we think of the writing process, we smell the dark roast and taste your baked oatmeal! Christie Babcock, Mara Brecht, Jean Donovan, and Tony Pichler: thanks for reading

drafts of the manuscript and offering thoughtful feedback and encouragement; in particular, thanks for engaging the text with your heads *and* hearts.

Finally, thanks to our spouses and families for being patient with us
through the years-long process of research and writing, and for pitching in
to make things work at our respective homes while we pursued this project.
To our daughters who at one point (jokingly, we hope) commiserated that
they had "lost their moms" to the book: the book is done, girls. We're all
yours. Be careful what you wish for.

We Are Not Meant to Be Alone

Authentic Friendship at the Heart of Marriage

"Find a friend." Jerry Simms calls it the "greatest piece of wisdom" he can offer on marriage. Jerry married his own "best friend," Lisa, fourteen years ago. They agree that their close friendship, established long before their wedding, is both at the heart of their marriage and essential to its success. When asked to describe their friendship, Lisa looked at Jerry and said, "When something really good happens or something really bad happens, you're the first person I want to tell about it." These friends enjoy spending time together and sharing the ins-and-outs of daily life. Jerry described the comfort and security that comes with a mutual knowing, accepting, and appreciating of "all of the little things" about each other. He looked at his wife: "I know what you like. I know what you don't like. I know your fears and am able to anticipate that and maybe help deal with it." Friendship—marked by deep intimacy, attentiveness, and delight in the other—is what Jerry and Lisa consider the bedrock of their marriage, the foundation upon which they raise their three sons.

Jerry and Lisa Simms are far from unique—again and again, we heard the language of friendship used to describe what partners appreciate about their spouse and what they celebrate within their marriage. Bill McCarthy, who has raised three children with his wife of twenty-six years, Katie, said that the best thing about marriage "is waking up with my best friend and going to bed and giving her a hug and kiss and thanking the Lord that I have her another day. There are frequent times I sit at work with all the pressures and struggles and I think to myself, *at the end of the day, when I go home, I'm going to be with my best friend again.* And to me, that's what keeps me going each and every day." Katie nodded, adding, "The longer we are married, the more I realize that he is my best friend. As the kids got older, it was easier for us as a couple to find that there was actually an identity to us as a couple that was not just two parents with three kids."

She recalled a recent trip that required three hours alone in the car to-gether followed by a weekend in close quarters. Rather than dreading the car ride and thinking, "Dang, I have to spend the whole weekend with my husband," Katie "couldn't wait." She explained a certain ease about their togetherness as they traveled, even when they were not talking. The ease that Katie describes typifies what well-known Christian scholar and writer, C. S. Lewis, calls affection [*storge*]. This love of affection, "besides being a love itself, can enter into other loves [*eros*, *philia*, and *caritas*] and color them all through."[1] Lewis believes "there is . . . a particular charm, both in friendship and in *eros*, about those moments when appreciative love lies, as it were, curled up asleep, and the mere ease and ordinariness of the rela-tionship (free as solitude, yet neither is alone) wraps us around. No need to talk. No need to make love. No needs at all except perhaps to stir the fire."[2]

Lewis's imagery is powerful. Spouses are wrapped in the "ordinariness of the relationship," taking great comfort in the presence of their old friend with whom they can fully relax. Katie's comments reflect an appreciation for the "charm" of the love that she shares with Jerry: "Easily he's my best friend. It's nice just being the two of us. I *like* being with him!"

Delight in the other is a great gift of friendship. This truth surfaced repeatedly in our interviews. For example, Beth Johnson, mother of seven young children, spoke enthusiastically about her husband: "What brings me joy is that Joe is really my best friend and has been since we've been dating. It makes me happy that I love him and respect him so much and that I can go to bed next to him, and I just want to be around him all the time. When we have free time, we try to plan things together. It makes me happy in life to be with someone who I want to be around, and who brings me up." She looked at Joe and said, "You think I am happy, but you help make me happy, you respect what I do."[3] Turning back to us, she said, "I respect him and his job . . . . He's my best friend, and it makes me happy to be around someone who is that uplifting and good."

In Beth's words, one hears admiration and gratitude for her friend who is good, who uplifts her and brings her joy. Similarly, Margaret Murphy—after twenty-six years of marriage—is struck by how much she enjoys her husband Matt's company: "We laugh together. We'll wake up in the middle of the night laughing together just about something stupid, or some joke someone told us; it's like all of a sudden, we'll both wake up and just start roaring or something." She laughed. "We both really have fun together. It can be at home, or we like a lot of the same things. We have similar interests. That brings me a lot of joy, just the companionship."

Couples noted that whether it is participating in shared interests, such as riding bikes or camping, or assisting each other with daily household tasks, such as washing the dishes: life is much more fun (or at least, when washing dishes, not so bad) with a friend.

The language of friendship is central to the way many couples in our study described their successful marriages. They used the words "friends" and "companions": friends—respecting, renewing, and supporting one another; companions—laughing, enjoying, and appreciating one another. Beyond the *frequency* of the language of friendship in the interviews, however, we recognize a *depth* to the way that friendship is described, as seen in the brief testimony above. In this chapter, we will examine friendship from a theological perspective. We will discuss the distinctiveness of Christian friendship, illustrated by the testimony of these couples.

Why We Need Friendship: Oh, the Pain Is Gone

The Christian tradition asserts that human beings are naturally social. In other words, God created us to live in communion, both with God and other people. This natural, God-given, sociality is reflected in the two creation stories in the Book of Genesis. In the creation account that appears first,[4] God simultaneously creates male and female in God's image and together names them *adam*.[5] In the second creation story, God creates the first human being (*adam*), but sees that the creature is lonely and in need of a partner. God declares: "It is not good that the man should be alone" (Gen 2:18). The animals cannot cure the creature's loneliness; the human needs a companion who is his equal, "bone of my bones and flesh of my flesh" (Gen 2:23). So God puts the human to sleep and creates male and female: two companions who unite to become "one flesh" (Gen 2:24).

We were reminded of this creation story when Thomas O'Brien told us about meeting Mary his wife of forty-two years, after spending thirty-nine years as a bachelor. "I went around most of my life doing all right, I was happy, I was contented, I thought I was doing a good job, with this kind of pain in my stomach, until I met Mary. *I never really knew what loneliness was until I met Mary.* I realized, [after meeting her] 'Oh the pain is gone!' I was free from this kind of lingering loneliness. That was a terrific gift for me, from her." Tom beautifully speaks of the gift he found in his partnership with Mary, a gift that freed him from a "lingering loneliness" that he tellingly describes as "pain." All of us who are made in God's image, like Tom, are made for communion.

Let us reflect for a moment here on the meaning of this core Christian anthropological claim: that is, human beings are made in God's image. Theologian Paul Wadell speaks simply but insightfully of the claim's implications when he writes: "human beings are created *from intimacy* and *for intimacy*."[6] He explains: "We are living, breathing images of a Trinitarian God whose very life is the fullness and perfection of intimacy. Born from this love, we are called to mirror in our lives the intimacy, friendship, and community we see perfectly displayed in God. *God is intimacy*. God—Father, Son, and Holy Spirit—is a perfect communion of love."[7] Because we are created in God's image, and because the very nature of God is loving communion, we will only flourish—that is, we will only live up to our potential as human beings—in intimate partnership with one another. We need friendship.

In *Happiness and the Christian Moral Life*, Wadell notes that "the moral importance of friendship and community is often overlooked."[8] While we surely enjoy and celebrate our friendships, we sometimes do not adequately appreciate the connection between having authentic friends and being a good person. Yet, philosophers such as Aristotle thought extensively about this connection, arguing that "a life of goodness and happiness depends on certain kinds of friendships."[9] If we are to live up to our potential as human beings, if we are to become virtuous, Aristotle insisted, we need good friends.

Christian thinkers like Thomas Aquinas agreed that we need friendship in order to be good, that being in a community of friends is essential to human flourishing. But Aquinas "radically reenvisioned" Aristotle's account of the centrality of friendship in the moral life "by suggesting that human beings are made not only for friendship with one another, but also for friendship with God—what he called charity or *caritas*. Our most exquisite happiness, Aquinas insisted, comes from all of us *together* seeking and enjoying a life of intimate friendship with God."[10] Not only then do our friends help us to be better persons, but they make us holy, bringing us closer to God. One thoughtful interviewee captured this strikingly as it relates to the married life: "Not only *our* marriage, but marriage in general, calls one to go beyond oneself—from self to other—and that journey, that direction, that momentum is what ultimately ends in God."

Becoming Holy through Married Friendship

But how exactly *does* married friendship make us holy? The testimony of couples in our study indicates that friendship in marriage brings partners closer to God in various ways, four of which we highlight here: it inspires virtue by example; it teaches self-transcendence and responsibility for the other; it leads to personal flourishing through support and challenge; and it strengthens partners to live out their faith commitments.

Inspiring by Example: He Is a Role Model

When children are moving through their school-aged years, it is not uncommon for parents to worry about the kinds of people their children befriend. On occasion, they might even gently suggest that their children end a friendship or find a new set of friends. Why? Because we know from experience that friends are highly influential in shaping one's character, for good or for ill. Aristotle argues that we *become* good by spending time with good people.[11] Good friends make us better; they rub off on us, so to speak. We admire the good qualities of our friends; we want to become like them (sometimes while fighting off the urge to ask them to stop making us look bad!). Simply put, "it is often in the company of our friends that we are reminded of the kind of person we want to become and the ideals and values that are important to us."[12]

For example, Anne Marie Donlan cried when telling us how her husband, Jim, makes her a better person. "Because he is such a good person. I don't want to let him down. . . . He is a role model for me to be a better parent because of his parenting and his care and concern for his family—not just us, but his extended family as well." Since Jim is "really good about calling his parents," it prompts Anne Marie to do the same. Moreover, his devotion to Anne Marie inspires her to be as devoted to him. "I see how hard he works . . . to be a good husband to me so I want to be that [same kind of spouse] to him." The example that Jim sets motivates Anne Marie to offer "constant prayer" in which she asks God: "How can I be a better mother? How can I be a better wife? How can I be a better friend?"

Carol Landry likewise uses the language of "role modeling" when extolling the good qualities of her husband of thirty-four years, Pat. Carol said, "Pat models attributes that aren't my strengths, like patience. If we're in a situation where I am just climbing the walls, Pat can be very levelheaded which makes me think (a) I should be doing that and (b) it can be done." Another woman noted that her husband is much better than she at saying sorry and forgiving, which "challenges [her] to be better at that," while she is more apt to be generous with their goods, which has caused her husband to more actively practice generosity.

After fifty-two years of marriage, Phil Rullo praises the virtues of his wife, Jane. "I like very much her patience and her capacity for forgiveness. . . . She has always been very respectful of who I am and what I do. I appreciate her great capacity to love. She's a very giving person, and *I try to reciprocate* that love because she is so generous with it."

Like Anne Marie and Carol above, Phil explicitly recognizes how his wife models particular virtues—in this case: patience, forgiveness, respect, love, and generosity—that, in turn, shape him and call him to be more virtuous. "Our marriage has made me a better person by helping me become a more patient person and an understanding person, and a great deal of that is a result of the kind of modeling that Jane does. I see her at work with others and interacting with others. I see the patience and understanding that she exhibits, and that certainly has helped me." Jane has been an *excellent* teacher for Phil in every sense of the word. Her goodness has helped to make him good.

In our conversations with couples, we heard many speak about being inspired by the characteristics and behaviors of their partners to become better spouses, and more fundamentally, better *people.* These few examples illustrate how spouses draw goodness out of one another by practicing virtues themselves.

Seeking the Good of the Other: Leave Your Ego at the Doorstep

Friendship calls us to be self-transcendent. It "draws us out of ourselves and challenges us to be attentive not to our own immediate interests and needs but to the interests and needs of another."[13] Indeed, day after day, friendship in marriage requires us to overcome self-centeredness and move toward other-centeredness. High school sweethearts Jim Donlan and his wife, Anne Marie, have been married twenty-nine years. Jim emphasized the self-transcendence prompted by his marriage:

> We're not meant to live by ourselves. I don't think it's an accident that it's in the Book of Genesis that we weren't alone for very long. And that makes you a better person because when you are completely alone, everything you do is completely centered on you. And so when I got married to Anne Marie, it wasn't me anymore. And boy, when we had kids, I looked through the nursery window and there was that little fat pink thing lying there and oh my God! Now it's not even just the two of us . . . I really don't think you can live up to the potential of how really good you can be by yourself. I

just really don't think you can. It's taking care of somebody, loving
somebody, raising somebody, burying somebody; I mean every step
along the way."

Jim recognizes and highlights the important connection between becoming
responsible to others—meeting the daily needs of his wife and children over
the long haul—and growth in goodness. If one is faithful to a friend "every
step of the way," one is inevitably challenged to grow ever more patient,
more loyal, more kind, more generous, and so on.

Wadell points out that "seeking the good of the other steadily and routinely" is far from easy. If we happen to be married, or have long-lasting
friendships, this is not news to us. In fact, seeking the good of the other consistently is "a high moral achievement, not the least because there are stubborn
tendencies in all of us to put ourselves first."[14] Lasting friendship therefore
requires *humility*, an attitude and corresponding behavior that displace oneself as the absolute center of concern. Humility is the virtue that counters
"stubborn tendencies" toward self-centeredness and the cultural messages of
radical individualism that reinforce them, but it must be nurtured.

For decades now, Pete and Sally Mahon have recited the Prayer of St.
Francis together daily. They included the prayer in their wedding Mass
and decided to make daily recitation of it a part of their married life. They
described lying in bed at night, asking the other, "Did we say our prayer yet?"
They have made the prayer their own, and it, in turn, has made something
of them—specifically, it teaches them to be humble. Sally explains that the
prayer "takes you out of yourself . . . it is not so much 'to be consoled as to
console.'" Sally also spoke of the special meaning that the Sermon on the
Mount, and in particular the Beatitudes, have for her: "There is so much
about humility. There has to be humility if you commit yourself to another
human being. We are difficult beings but . . . there is so much in there about
forgiveness and being humble and not always being right. I definitely have
a bigger issue with being stubborn and being right, but it's [the Sermon on
the Mount] that calls me to [be otherwise]—and I know I am much happier
when I don't have to be right, or I [try to be] humble or meek."

In the same vein, Jane Rullo beautifully describes how her fifty-two-year
marriage has demanded humility, and how practicing humility has benefited
both her and her husband:

> Prior to my marriage, I probably had been a little selfish. I had been
> an only child. When you get married, you realize in many ways you
> are responsible for that other human being. Not that you become

their parent—I don't mean that. But they become that most important person in your life. That you are no longer the most important
person and that you took that vow because you loved them in a way
that you loved no other human being. And thus, you really want
that person to become the best that they could become. And I think
that's what marriage has done. It has made me want another human
being to become the very best they can become and I worked very
hard on that. And I learned that things don't always go your way.
I always used to think I was right all the time. And I learned I was
not right all the time and that you had to give a little and, in turn,
that other person gave a little. It was both people working together
to make each other better.

In their twenty-eight years of marriage, Jack and Gretchen Baker have
endured the death of a child and raised two sons. Jack said the following:
"How does a marriage get strong? How do you keep building it? I think
it's when you finally realize that it is not about you. It's about them. Each
of you starts focusing on the other—it's about making *them* happy, pleasing
them." As did Jane Rullo, Jack stressed the importance of *mutually* seeking
the good of the other, noting that "when you're both doing that, it's easy."

We heard the same message from many other couples as well. One wife
practices daily reflection on what will make her husband happy: "I want
him to be happy; it's not about what he can do for me." What will make a
person happy is *particular to that person* and depends on knowing that person
intimately. As Jerry Simms noted above, he is better able to meet his wife's
needs because he knows the "little things" about her—her likes and dislikes,
and her fears. Anne Marie Donlan regularly prays in order to know how to
rightly love her husband in light of life's changes and challenges: "I have to
remind myself that just because that's the way I would handle something,
it's not exactly what he needs."

Attending to the needs and desires of one's partner often looks like
trying to see a situation from the other's point of view, "compromising,"
and "letting go of the need to be right all the time." In light of this reality,
theologian Richard Gaillardetz suggests that partners are converted within
marriage on a daily basis through the "experience of being stretched by the
otherness of one's spouse."[15] He concludes that this is "nothing less than
God's saving work in us."[16]

In other words, learning to care for one's spouse, who is radically other,
changes one for the better, helping one move away from sin and selfishness and toward holiness and goodness. It is, simply, conversion through

friendship. Gaillardetz draws on a biblical term, *kenosis*, or self-emptying, to name what is demanded of married partners in this process of conversion. He writes: "Saint Paul used the term [*kenosis*] to describe what it was for Christ to abandon all divine prerogatives in order to enter fully into the experience of being human. For those who fulfill our baptismal call to follow Jesus in and through the sacrament of matrimony, *kenosis* is the call to a self-emptying or dying to our own needs, hopes, and expectations."[17] *Kenosis* in marriage demands letting go of pride in order to compromise or put the other's wants first (in large or small matters—from how to discipline a child to where to go out to eat). And it sometimes calls for significant self-sacrifice.[18]

Jane Rullo's husband, Phil, suggested that self-sacrifice is one of the virtues necessary for a successful marriage, explaining that "you have to leave your ego at the doorstep when you get married, really. You have to have a friendship, [that requires] . . . losing your egocentricity and losing your selfishness and gaining a kind of selflessness. If there is anything important in marriage, it is putting selfishness aside, becoming selfless, and being willing to sacrifice for someone else."[19]

Joe Johnson, whose wife praised him as her best friend, said: "What comes to mind for me is what Jesus says, that there is no greater act of love than to lay down one's life for a friend. When you get over your own ego and selfishness and everything *you* want, you realize life is so much better when you're giving of yourself."

We want to emphasize that upholding self-sacrifice as an ideal in marriage can be problematic if *equality* and *justice* are not present. Catholic ethicist Margaret Farley argues that loving relationships (such as married relationships) ought to be characterized by justice, and she rightly warns that "[w]hen a disproportionate burden of sacrifice is laid on one person in a commitment-relationship, and when the person who bears it is the one with the least power, the duty of self-sacrifice is morally suspect."[20] An emphasis on self-sacrifice for those who lack equality of power may be destructive of their flourishing rather than constructive of it. Theologian Herbert Anderson helpfully highlights the connection between self-sacrifice, justice, and mutuality in marriage:

> Compromise [in marriage] is inevitable. No one can "have it all" if marriage is to be just. And no one does all the accommodating if the love is mutual. The deeper meaning of sacrifice is not about giving up our freedoms or our preferences but giving them over to a larger reality. That larger reality is a marriage of love **and** justice.

> If both partners in a marriage are committed to a just relationship,
> then no one person will do all of the accommodating. . . . If both
> husband and wife are committed to forming a just marriage, then the
> willingness to set aside our needs for the needs of others becomes a
> positive expression of a common bond. Sacrifice deepens a marital
> bond as long as each person in a relationship is committed to justice.
> When one partner does all the accommodating or when the sacrifices
> are not evenly distributed over time, the marriage is not just.[21]

In our interviews, we heard couples both praise mutual self-sacrifice and
express an awareness of the possibility of injustice when sacrifice is one-
sided. For example, Sally Mahon noted her husband's tendency to habitually give way to her and insightfully said, "I need to be careful not to take
advantage of his good nature."

We argue that self-sacrifice will be most fruitful in marriage when: equality is respected in the relationship; it is mutual (that is, expected of both
partners); and both spouses have a well-developed sense of self. It is unjust
for one person to consistently concede to the other's desires/needs/dreams
at the expense of her or his own.

Supporting and Encouraging One Another: Go Ahead, Go Ahead

Married friends build one another up through support and encouragement. In light of her own qualitative study of longtime married couples,
psychologist Judith Wallerstein concluded that *providing emotional nurturance
is essential to a good marriage.*[22] Married partners provide much-needed
comfort and encouragement for one another as they move through their days
together. When spouses face pressure at work and, if they have children,
stress in the home as they balance childcare and day-to-day household tasks,
it is easy to feel "not good enough," even overwhelmed. Married friends
rely on one another for emotional replenishment and reinforcement—we
saw this illustrated above, when Bill McCarthy expressed such relief in returning to his best friend at the end of a demanding day at work. In dealing
with daily stresses, and especially when facing failures, big or small—for
example, getting passed over for a raise; botching an important presentation
to colleagues; screaming at the children when patience is lost—"men and
women alike need a person they trust who reassures them, saying 'You did
the best you could,' who alleviates their worry, saying confidently, 'You
couldn't help it, so why blame yourself?' and who sends them back to battle
with the message 'You can do it, really you can.'"[23]

Al and Christine Kozak, who are married twenty years and raising five children, spoke compellingly about the efforts that they make to build one another up. Al said, "Confidence would be a good word for me [to describe this]. Being able to confide in her, the encouragement, it goes both ways. Small example: she started a new business recently, and I did little things, whether send her a note, or bring some flowers before her first show, just to say, 'Hey, you're doing the right thing.' And it goes back and forth . . . it could be a small note, or sending a text in the middle of the day, to help." The couple emphasized the importance of boosting each other's self-esteem in very concrete ways—whether it be through spoken words, gestures, or texts. "We encourage each other . . . it helps us be successful as a married couple."

Al noted that mutual encouragement is particularly important in challenging times: "There will be times that we're knocked down. We're not always going to be the tallest guy on the platform. Something's going to happen—maybe you didn't get a job, or you didn't get a promotion, or you didn't make a sale. You try to get an article published if you're a writer, like she's done so many times—maybe it didn't go as well, whatever it could be, but you have to have a strong self-esteem," and so they work to support one another.

Christine emphasized the importance of intimate knowledge of your spouse in order to meet his or her needs in this regard. "You have to know your spouse, when [he or she] could be at a low, and [he or she] needs a little bit more encouragement or motivation or a little boost of confidence, for whatever reason, because everyone needs that. And you have to be aware of that and you have to be able to say, 'Hey, you did a good job on this.'"

Wallerstein explains that "[s]elf-esteem is not a single idea; rather, it is like a tripod whose three legs are feeling loved, feeling virtuous, and feeling competent. If all three are strong, they support high self-esteem and self-confidence."[24] This tripod of self-esteem "is challenged every day of our lives. We give ourselves new grades with each important experience."[25]

Depending on what happens at work or at home, we might feel successful and competent, or we might feel inadequate and like a failure. Our spouse plays an important role, helping us to see ourselves more clearly by reminding us of our gifts and abilities, by reminding us that we are competent, good, and loved. In the words of Al and Christine: "Hey, you're doing the right thing," and "Hey, you're good at this." Or maybe most importantly, "Hey, no matter what, at the end of the day, you are loved."

Donna Erikson described the support that she received from Tim her husband of thirty-two years when her business venture failed, which was a devastating loss: "I said [to Tim], 'You can't fix this, I've got to work on it.

Just love me through it, that's all I ask. Just be there and love me through it.' And he did."

Knowing that our spouse loves us and believes in us allows us to take risks that we may not otherwise seize, a powerful gift of friendship.[26] Kathleen and Jeremy Cotter's story is full of risk-taking. They were married in a traditional peacekeeping church and raised their children in an intentional community, sharing goods and values with others, becoming a kind of extended family. It was a wonderful experience in many ways, but at some point, Kathleen and Jeremy became restless. Kathleen began looking for something different spiritually. In her searching, she wandered into a Catholic church. Here is how she describes her journey:

> I was basically feeling spiritually crawling-through-the-desert-thirsty, needing depth in my faith walk, really desperately needing depth and reading [Henri] Nouwen and [Thomas] Merton and stuff. And I had always been intrigued by Catholicism, since way back my family is actually Irish Catholic but, through a long series of stories, wasn't by the time I came along. So I always wanted to see what was going on in that big church up here [in the parish they eventually joined]. So one day . . . I came in and came to Mass . . . and it answered so much for me . . . I found the depth I was looking for.
>
> In terms of our marriage, *this is what is really critical*: Jeremy was cool with that. I mean, this was a big deal. We'd been living in this intentional community and to do something this much outside the box was like, woo!, [even though] we were both ready to be leaving anyway, we knew that was probably going to happen, but I just did it first. I really did feel completely supported in figuring this out. Go ahead! Go ahead! And that was fabulous, absolutely fabulous, to have not just support but *faith* in my mind and my spirit, to know that I was not just crazy, you know? It's a big deal. And eventually he came too.

What is striking here is the support that Jeremy offered to Kathleen in her search—go ahead! go ahead!—that allowed her to take a real risk, a risk that they both knew might result—and in fact *did* result—in a radical change for their whole family. Jeremy offered "faith in [her] mind and [her] spirit" that gave Kathleen the courage to explore what would best quench her thirst and bring her closer to God. As noted, eventually both Kathleen and Jeremy joined the Catholic parish into which she "wandered" and converted to Catholicism. They found a community that enriches them, but only because Jeremy encouraged Kathleen to take a chance. Kathleen said, "The whole thing about marriage, our marriage, but also marriage more broadly, is that it's a safe place to take risks. We are able to take risks together, for example, leaving the intentional community . . . and actually at one point in our lives, we both quit our jobs, when we had two kids in college. And we both knew this was the right thing to do, and somehow we could just do that."

A similar story was told by a man who, after becoming inspired by a talk at church about using one's gifts for God and other people, went home and told his wife that he would like to quit his job. "She said, 'Are you sure?' I said, 'Yeah.' That's all she said. She smiled and just accepted it. It's a great wife that will let you go with what you think you want to do." His wife added, "He didn't tell you the whole thing. The whole thing is that he said he wanted to do work for God and we both knew we would live on less than half his salary . . . and I said, 'yes.'" Incidentally, the couple was raising eight children together.

In these cases—changing church affiliation, quitting jobs—spouses supported their partner in following what seemed to be a call from God to live more fully and deeply. Kathleen said, "[W]e weren't playing it safe. And I think our marriage has made it easier. I don't know what I would have done by myself, but, you know, the tendency might have been to play it safe a little more. That is directly related to getting closer to God. You can't do that stuff without it bringing you closer to God."

Clearly, mutual encouragement between these married friends opened up a space for risk-tasking, allowing the partners to more freely and fully engage in the world. Safety lies in the fact that, if the risk does not turn out well, blame and shame need not take over; rather, partners can move on with life together, loving one another through it, as Donna and Tim Erikson did when her business failed.

We are not suggesting, of course, that it is good to support every whim expressed by one's spouse, but rather that it is good to assist one's partner in discernment, helping him or her see oneself and one's goals more clearly, and support the other's deepest desires. Prudence—or, practical decision-making—is crucial, and prudence demands discernment. Repeatedly, we heard from spouses about how helpful it is to honestly discuss their anxieties, hopes, and desires together, thereby discerning *in partnership and in a continuing way*: who they are, what is important to them, and where they are going in light of their commitments. In this process, we see friends learn about themselves, see themselves ever more clearly in and through their spouse, and find the courage to follow their vocations.

Challenging One Another: I Prefer to Call It Caringly Direct

Supporting and encouraging one another—building each other up—is one important way that spouses help each other move toward their potential. Yet, spouses do not only serve as conversation partners, encouragers, and cheerleaders, rightfully reminding their partners of their many gifts and talents. Sometimes the work of intimacy involves revealing to one's spouse the ways he or she needs to grow, which may be met with resistance. After all, we love to hear the many good things that our spouses see and admire in us, but comments about our negative tendencies and behaviors are not as welcome. Nevertheless, "because all of us have only limited knowledge of ourselves, and sometimes the little we do know is tainted by self-deception," we need friends to see ourselves more clearly, "including aspects of ourselves we might prefer not to know."[27]

Since we are all imperfect, many spouses talked about "choosing battles" and "overlooking" the weaknesses in their partners in the day-to-day grind of married life, which is healthy and realistic. It is readily apparent that nitpicking and tearing down one's spouse for every offense or flaw is harmful and destructive of relationship. Thus, a marriage must be marked by a generosity of spirit in order to flourish. On the other hand, when necessary, spouses are obligated to point out negative behavior and flaws in their partner that rightly should change. After all, true friends are committed to helping one another live up to their potential. This commitment is captured beautifully in a phrase that we heard repeatedly: "Our job is to get each other to heaven."

Jeff and Laura Rader—married thirty-four years, with three grown children and "lots of granddaughters"—discussed the sometimes tough work of friendship in their marriage. Jeff said, "She challenges me to grow and can be blunt with me sometimes—which is good." Laura responded: "I prefer to call it caringly direct." They laughed. She added: "Jeff makes me a better person because he points out things to me as well. Not as bluntly, but . . . [more laughter] he challenges me to grow in the virtues. I can only change myself so he can highlight those [areas of growth] for me. But I know that at the end of the day, or the end of the conversation, or the end of him pointing out my faults or an area I need to grow in, he is going to love me through it, so I have a comfort foundation that even when I'm not perfect he loves me and that's good. That's a blessing."

Early in our conversation with the Raders, Laura stated that Jeff's unconditional love for her is "the foundation of my life, and I think that's the foundation of our marriage." In the extended quote above, Laura is quick to point out that their unconditional love for each other creates a safe space to point out certain weaknesses and opportunities for growth. They can offer and receive constructive criticism because they are confident that the other will "love [them] through it."

It may be a small moment when a spouse calls the other out on inappropriate behavior that can nevertheless make a lasting impact. One man recalled that, early in his marriage, he was impatient with a store clerk who seemed new to the job and was fumbling as she served him. When the couple left the store, the wife immediately reprimanded her husband for his impatience and lack of compassion for the clerk. Through the years, when he has felt like expressing impatience, he remembers what his wife said about the store clerk and instead tries to be more understanding.

Relatedly, sometimes spouses help one another set boundaries in light of unhealthy tendencies. For example, one wife of an engineer identified her husband's weakness as "wanting to work all the time," so she reminds him of the importance of setting limits. Another man, whose tendency is to take on too many responsibilities, is grateful that his wife straightforwardly tells him, "You can't take that on." He appreciates that his wife brings balance to his life so that he does not overextend and "head straight toward burnout."

In both of these cases, the spouse helped the partner see and avoid negative tendencies. One woman, who is about to celebrate twenty years of marriage with her spouse, said: "I love my husband because he knows me better than I know myself sometimes. He kind of keeps me in check and keeps me grounded. Sometimes all I need is a look or a phrase and then, I'm like, 'okay, I got it.'" Those of us who have been married long enough are likely familiar with, and (ultimately) appreciative of, "the look" that keeps us in check, from the one who knows us better than we know ourselves.

Tom and Nancy Brady, who have been married for twenty-one years and are raising four children, spoke beautifully about how love—the love between spouses and the love of God—creates a safe space for them to acknowledge and deal with weakness. Nancy notes that sometimes when she is talking to her husband about daily struggles, she realizes her own "bad points" or "areas that [she] needs to work on to become a better person." In this case, her husband is not pointing out these weaknesses directly; instead, she discovers them and can be honest about them in conversation with him. She believes that if she were not married, she would "sulk within herself" about these negative aspects of herself. But having her husband to talk with her about it and gaining his perspective gives her a better understanding of who she is and what she needs to do to "trust in [her] faith" and deal with her faults.

Tom builds on Nancy's reflections, explaining that the two of them hold each other accountable. "There is an accountability there. I don't mean that in a business sense, but there is an obligation, or accountability to each other. I need her; she needs me; we need each other; we need the Lord. It's an interdependence that in our world today may sound negative." Tom thinks that honoring interdependence is countercultural insofar as our culture prizes radical independence, especially for men. Yet Tom "refuse[s] to play the macho game," freely admitting: "I can't do this alone. It's humility. I need her and I need the Lord." Nancy emphasizes that mutual dependence is important when one needs to confront one's faults "barefaced": "If you didn't have that other person by your side and then have God with his arms wrapped around the two of you, you would never get through to the point where you could become a better person."

Living Faith Together: Are You a Christian, Or Not?

Thomas O'Brien has had a successful career that inadvertently put him in daily contact with people in need of resources. He was "getting calls from people who did not know what to do. Their welfare checks had been cut off or they were being sued by their landlords and kicked out of their houses. Over a period of time, [Thomas] was gathering lawyers and social workers and such agencies to put in touch with them." Thomas recalled a time when he was complaining to his wife, Mary, about the burden of serving all these people, and Mary said, "Well, what do you expect? Are you a Christian, or not?" The questions posed by Mary reminded Thomas of his responsibility as a Christian to serve the needs of the poor and vulnerable, even when inconvenient. To refuse their pleas when Thomas was capable of responding to them would be to reject his own highest aspirations.

Good friends help us stay committed to what is most important to us, just as Mary did for Thomas. Wadell explains: "No matter how worthwhile a project or activity might be, if we are left to pursue it alone it is easy to grow discouraged and indifferent."[28] For Christians, living out our baptisms and becoming closer to God ought to be the most important (though not always the easiest) project of our lives. It is a project we must embark on together, for we are baptized *into community*. It is important to remember that, in the Gospels, the disciples were sent out "two by two" in order to spread the good news with their words and their lives.

Couples who completed our written survey overwhelmingly confirm the importance of shared morals, values, and faith in the success of their marriage. Specifically, 98 percent of respondents consider shared morals/values to be important to their marriage. In addition, 98 percent believe that sharing a core set of faith beliefs is important. These married partners recognize that when they live out shared faith and values *together*, they are stronger for it. In an interview, one husband confirmed the importance of the core faith beliefs shared with his wife, that—he explained to us—are rooted in the faith lives of their respective families of origin: "We have the same values, which is nice. Both of us sharing the same values makes life a lot easier. We have different ideas about some things, but in general, we're both going in the same direction, you know, bringing our family along for the ride."

Pete Mahon talked about the importance of a shared faith with his wife, Sally: "Before Sally, I dated a girl for a while, a really nice girl, but she wasn't Catholic, and there was always that question mark. And sharing that same faith is a huge value to have because it is a tough enough world out there, [and tougher] if you don't start from the same spot—now we may problem-solve differently, but at least we can start from that same spot—using a baseball analogy, from home plate. Since we were both blessed to have that same faith, that is a huge deal."

His wife responded, "I would agree, but I don't necessarily think you'd need to both be Catholic. I think that would be a good thing, but I also can see situations where there are two Catholic people . . . it's all about how much your faith in God matters to you. If one of you had a pretty fervent faith and the other was like 'Yeah, I was raised Catholic,' but it didn't matter much, then it's not going to [be a shared priority]. But faith for both of us was a priority."

Since faith is a priority for both Pete and Sally, they consider it the home plate for all of their endeavors—the source from which they go out into the world and to which they return, safely. Thus they actively nurture and deepen that faith, together and as individuals, by praying daily, trying to make it to daily Mass, attending yearly retreats, and participating in Scripture reflection and faith-sharing groups. These practices allow them to "keep checking in with God" and "keep them on their game."

Donna Erikson explained how partnership and mutual encouragement have functioned to strengthen the faith of each spouse in their married life:

> We've done so many things together, you know, Marriage Encounter and all kinds of prayer groups and different things that we do together. Even our first reconciliation. When we were growing

up, we didn't make that, it wasn't in the church—or wasn't in our
parish, which was pretty contemporary—so we were married seven
years and we were in church and they had the opportunity to go
[to reconciliation] face-to-face and we were going, "Should we?"
and I am sure if I was in there by myself I wouldn't have, but when
you have each other we [said], "Yeah, okay, let's do it." So we encourage each other. You know one goes on a retreat and you fill up
the other one and then the other one does something, and we fill
each other up. Right now we've been doing this Oremus[30] and it's
been kind of cool because we read [part of the Bible] and then we
can talk about, "What hit you in that Scripture, that piece? And,
where were you at?," and it's just kind of fun to do that. We really
do help each other get closer to God.

Notice the language that Donna uses here: the language of encouragement.
She and her husband, Tim, genuinely *give one another courage* in their faith
journey. The Latin root word of courage is *cor*, or "heart." Recall that Wadell
notes how easy it is to become *dis*couraged, that is, to lose heart, when
pursuing the most important goals of our lives. For this reason, we need
friends to give us courage, or enable us "to take heart."

Donna believes that she would have been too afraid to participate in the
sacrament of reconciliation had Tim not been with her. They were bolstered
by each other's presence in church that day—it made them brave enough to
engage—and it is only one example of their pursuit together of activities that
strengthen their faith. But even when one spouse pursues an activity as an
individual, such as going on retreat, it functions to encourage and "fill up"
the other, keeping the couple focused on what is most important to them.

Donna and Tim's experience was echoed by many who expressed profound gratitude for a spouse who strongly encouraged (and enabled) them
to go on retreat, or perhaps to join and continue regularly meeting with
a parish group, indicating that they "would never" have taken that step
without some prodding from their partner.[31]

Matthew Murphy told us that he and his wife, Margaret, share a favorite
biblical passage, which is "when Jesus unrolls the scroll and reads from
Isaiah[32] and then puts it down and says, 'Today the scriptures are fulfilled
in your presence.' And then they chase him to the top of the mountain and
try to kill him right after that. But that's part of [it]." Matthew appreciates
the "passion for justice" that is revealed in Jesus' words—about proclaiming good news to the poor, restoring sight to the blind, and setting the
prisoners and oppressed free. Yet Matthew also highlighted the rejection

of Jesus by the crowds that followed his message, and said, "I don't think I could even do or think of that [i.e., the kind of justice Jesus proclaimed and lived] without having a partner in that." He looked at his wife. "You're sometimes pushing me along in that, and sometimes just giving me the courage to speak up and take a stand on certain things. Not that I do a lot of that, but I would do a lot less, I think, if I weren't married to Margaret."

From the testimony we heard, it seems true that these married partners would "do a lot less" to live out their most cherished Christian ideals if they were not married; their shared faith commitments and the encouragement of their spouse to enact those values enables them to do more.

The way that Matthew speaks about Margaret pushing him to live out gospel values—to challenge an unjust status quo—points to the fact that friendships are "potentially subversive—acts of genuine protest and resistance—because they dare to break free from what is most corrupting and dehumanizing in a culture in order to begin something new."[33] Above, it was suggested that Christian marriage is countercultural because it celebrates the inherently social nature of the person and our consequent interdependence, rather than touting radical individualism and independence.

Further, we noted the necessity of humility in marriage, of self-emptying service to the other, modeled after Jesus Christ. Humility and self-emptying service not only contrast cultural messages of individualism—with its "me-first" mentality—but also consumerism and materialism, that teach us to fill ourselves up with the latest gadgets and goods, even at the expense of others in our communities. Wadell names the narrative of consumerism and materialism and the narrative of individualism, "narratives of despair" because they have a dehumanizing effect on us. Rather than helping us live to our potential, they distort our full humanity.[34]

To this list of narratives of despair, he adds "the narrative of violence," that he sees "at work in a culture that so prizes competition and rivalry that it teaches us that the only way we can secure our own identity is by dominating and oppressing somebody else."[35]

Authentic friendship, then, is subversive because—together—friends can reject these narratives of despair and choose to live differently, in ways that are more truthful and hopeful. Friends can help free one another from the corrupting effects of these false narratives. We vividly saw *friendship as resistance* in the lives of the married couples to whom we spoke.

Bob and Jeanne Mitchell have made a commitment to live simply. They are "cautious" to resist "materialism and consumerism." Jeanne said, "[Living simply and sharing what we have] are things we value strongly, and value because we're called to those things—generosity and putting people ahead of things—and so we both value those and find those things difficult in different ways, and doing that together makes it more likely to get to the things we think are important."

Bob and Jeanne are helping one another stay committed to what is most important to them. They are living intentionally in a countercultural way by rejecting narratives of despair and choosing instead to adhere to gospel values, that they acknowledge can be "difficult." Jeanne's language of prioritizing "people ahead of things" reminds us of Pope St. John Paul II's call for Christians to emphasize *being* over *having* in *Sollicitudo Rei Socialis* (On Social Concern).[36]

Pope John Paul II condemns both economic underdevelopment and its counterpart, superdevelopment, "which consists in an excessive availability of every kind of material goods for the benefit of certain social groups" (SRS 28). The Pope charges that underdevelopment and superdevelopment are "equally inadmissible" because each is "contrary to what is good and to true happiness" (SRS 28). The danger specific to superdevelopment is that:

> [It] easily makes people slaves of "possession" and of immediate gratification, with no other horizon than the multiplication or continual replacement of the things already owned with others still better. This is the so-called civilization of "consumption" or "consumerism," which involves so much "throwing-away" and "waste." An object already owned but now superseded by something better is discarded, with no thought of its possible lasting value in itself, nor of some other human being who is poorer. . . . All of us experience firsthand the sad effects of this blind submission to pure consumerism: in the first place a crass materialism, and at the same time a radical dissatisfaction, because one quickly learns—unless one is shielded from the flood of publicity and the ceaseless and tempting offers of products—that the more one possesses the more one wants, while deeper aspirations remain unsatisfied and perhaps even stifled (SRS 28).

The Pope explains that in a superdeveloped country like the United States, those who are privileged and steeped in the narratives of consumerism and materialism often confuse *having* with *being*. We begin to believe that our worth and happiness are tied to the excessive goods we accumulate (our fancy cars, clothes, and houses), often at the expense of those who lack even basic material goods. We forget that material goods are meant to be shared and to serve the well-being of persons whose *real* happiness consists in virtuous living and right relationship with God and others. We are tricked by the narratives of despair so that our "deeper aspirations remain unsatisfied and perhaps even stifled." Therefore, it is imperative that Christians *resist*, and as Jeanne rightly points out, "doing that together makes it more likely to get to the things we think are important."

Frank and Kelly Brown both served in the Jesuit Volunteer Corps (JVC) after college and have adopted the "four cornerstones" of the JVC as the foundation of their marriage: simple living, social justice, community, and spirituality. These parents of three young children consider these values to be "anchors" or "hooks to hang so much of our life on," and claim that these cornerstones have been important in their "conversations and growth" as they have moved through their nineteen years of marriage. Kelly explained, "We want to live our life in a way that matters. That has been our grounding. [Our marriage] is about us, but it has been about more than us."

Frank and Kelly make concrete choices, big and small, that reflect these core values. For example, they intentionally choose to live in a condominium rather than buy a house in the urban community in which they live, which frees them to financially support community organizations and do service work, such as running a food pantry, supporting at-risk youth through housing and educational support, and teaching. They see the "choice to live simply as a way to be closer to God as a family." They are explicit about the motivation for such choices with their children, hoping to pass along these values to them. Kelly emphasizes that "we've always supported one another and encouraged each other in [living out their four values] and made the sacrifices that are required as well." In friendship, Kelly and Frank protest the dominant values of American culture with their very lives.

Al and Christine Kozak emphasize cooperation and teamwork in their home, where they are raising their five children. Countering the rampant individualism in our culture, Christine identifies herself primarily as part of a unit: "I just think of *us*, because we've known each other so long, it's like left foot, right foot, Al and Christine." Right foot, left foot: it is *one body* imagery.[37] Al described "an epiphany" he had after his wife delivered twin babies, and the couple was juggling work and family responsibilities. He realized, "There's just no way you can get everything done at this house. It's just impossible." Although at that time Christine was a mother who stayed at home full time, Al committed himself to helping out more around the house and with the children, in addition to working full time: "If you're going to make it work, you can't just put it all on one person's shoulders. You've got to divvy that up. In our culture now, people talk about being on a team, but [authentic teamwork] is actually countercultural because in education you get an individual report card and in the work environment typically you get a performance appraisal on you . . . really it's about the individual, even if we use the language of being a team. For our family, we have to do things as a team."

Al recalls a conversation that they had with their children at the dinner table when Christine was going back to part-time work outside the home. Al and Christine told the children that the change "means we're all going to have to help out. If we all help out, we'll still be able to have a lot of good times together, but everybody's going to have to pick it up a little bit." Al and Christine see each other—and the wider family—as a team, and they talk to their children regularly about helping out in whatever ways they are able in order to make their household function, but also to instill the values of helping others and being responsible to a common good. Rather than "competition and rivalry," the children are learning cooperation and responsibility to the group. Al teaches them: "If you help somebody, I call it the boomerang effect; it comes back. If you help people, it comes back ten times that. And that's what God wants you to do."

Al spoke, too, about a willingness to ask God for help in prayer. In Al's mind, God expects a great deal from them as parents of five children, but God is also there to help: "Sometimes people think it is on themselves to do it all themselves. For whatever reason, when you ask for help, people think that's a sign of weakness. To me, it's a sign of strength because you realize that you need that help."

In conclusion, we are convinced that married friends delight in the other, support and challenge one another, want and do what is best for the other, and—most fundamentally—share in the common project of bringing each other more deeply into friendship with God. We therefore affirm the excellent advice offered by Jerry Simms at the beginning of the chapter: marry a friend!

2

Erotic Love and Marriage

Making Love Twenty-Four Hours a Day

"We are sexual beings and that's a fact. That's who we are," said Ed Rorholm, husband of fifty-five years and father of eight. In light of our sexual nature, Ed argues, spouses should seriously contemplate and openly communicate about how sexuality impacts their marital relationship. We concur, and we believe a good starting point for married partners, as well as for this chapter, is to consider the anthropological assertion: *we are sexual beings*. Christian sexual ethicist Marvin Ellison defines sexuality as follows: "Sexuality is our embodied sensuality and capacity for connection. It is more than an isolated segment of our lives. It extends far beyond genital expression. Persons are body-selves. We connect with the world through our senses and through touch . . . sexuality is a mode of communication, the giving and receiving of recognition and regard. The erotic desire for knowledge—to know and be known by the other—goes far beyond the intellect or the genitals."[1] Ellison's definition of sexuality emphasizes our embodied desire and "capacity for connection," and helpfully notes that sexual interaction between partners is expressed in many different ways, including, but not limited to, genital expression.

Kyle Estus, a father of seven who has been married for forty-eight years, affirmed Ellison's inclusive definition of sexuality during a focus group, saying, "What is sexuality? It is not necessarily the actual act [of sexual intercourse]. It can be just looking at each other, holding hands, or just treating someone especially kind or nice, that's all part of it, and it gives you a lot of good feeling." Kyle's remark illustrates that a tender look, a gentle touch, and a kind interaction are indeed expressions of sexuality, ways of "giving and receiving of recognition and regard," that express and increase connection between two embodied spouses.

One woman told us about a habitual night-time routine with her husband, that she believes helps them "stay connected": "We say good night to each other; we say 'I love you,' give each other a kiss and have some kind of contact when we're falling asleep, whether it's a head on a shoulder or feet touching. It's just those little things, even though you are sleeping, you are spending that time together."

Those little things. Words of affirmation spoken. A kiss. A head on a shoulder. Feet touching. In Kyle's words, *that's all part of it.* Simply put, these examples from ordinary, married life are expressions of erotic love.

In chapter 1, we discussed primarily the love known as *philia.* Our conversations with married couples convinced us that authentic friendship is at the heart of marriage. But married partners, we know, are not "just friends." Or, better, they are special kinds of friends because in marriage (ideally) the love of friendship, *philia*, is combined with *eros*, or romantic love. Note that Ellison uses the language of the erotic (root word *eros*) in his definition of sexuality above. Admittedly, the word erotic may be off-putting to some insofar as it is commonly associated with what is pornographic (think erotic bookstores or films). But we need not be afraid of this way of thinking and talking about love if it is rightly understood. *Eros* is a love that is rooted in passion and desire. It is the desire to be united with the beloved—not only, or even primarily, through sex. C. S. Lewis describes *eros* as the state of being in love. Lewis takes for granted that *eros* "includes other things besides sexual activity."[2] Theologian Sallie McFague explains that the crux or core of erotic love is not lust but rather *value*: "It is in finding someone else valuable and being found valuable."[3] A lover thinks, "I love you just because you are you, I delight in your presence, you are precious beyond all saying to me," and therefore I want to be united with you.[4] I want to be connected to you. I want to be one with you.

The passion and desire for unification that is inherent in erotic love is wonderfully described by the medieval Sufi poet Rumi:

> Lovers share a sacred decree—
>   to seek the Beloved.
>   They roll head over heels,
> rushing toward the Beautiful One
>   like a torrent of water.[5]

Passionately seeking the beloved is identified by Rumi as "sacred," implying that *eros* can be a holy kind of love, whether the beautiful one is another person, such as one's spouse, or the Beautiful One is God. The medieval mystics of the Christian tradition understood this and were not shy about referring to God as Lover.[6] For example, Julian of Norwich, fourteenth-century mystic, suggests, "God wants to be thought of as our Lover. I must see myself so bound in love as if everything that has been done has been done for me. That is to say, the Love of God makes such a unity in us that when we see this unity, no one is able to separate oneself from another."[7]

Sallie McFague's description of erotic love applies here: Julian of Norwich refers to a zealous love that is fundamentally about unification with the beloved. Love binds us not only to God but also to one another—so closely that we become inseparable. It calls to mind the *one body* imagery of Genesis (discussed in chapter 1), that is applied in the Christian tradition both to married couples and to the wider church as Body of Christ. We are bound so tightly together in God that we become one body, one living thing. Married partners become one body in the sacrament of matrimony and, ideally, express and deepen that unity through their sexual relationship.

Holy Sex!: It's Healthy and It's Wonderful!

Lisa Landwehr, a mother of five who has been married for forty-two years, claims that "a healthy sex life within marriage is very important.[8] We live in a society that is so overexposed to sexuality. It is all around us all the time, but the focus on healthy sexuality is not there. It's all dirty. If we could get back to how important a healthy sex life is within a marriage, couples would realize that it's wonderful; it isn't something that our society is telling us. It's healthy and it's wonderful."

In our conversations with couples, Lisa was far from alone in lamenting the limited or false ways that our society presents sexuality and relationships. For example, Joe Johnson regrets that in our culture sex is narrowly presented as purely "recreational" and "free from consequences," whereas the Christian tradition teaches that sex "creates obligations and connections," as C. S. Lewis nicely put it.[9] Joe's wife, Beth, agrees with her husband, noting that sex is often portrayed as "recreational and diversional . . . but it doesn't necessarily have a spiritual dimension to it."

To be sure, American culture is sex-saturated—as Lisa points out, we are "overexposed" to sexual imagery. The media both reflects and shapes a culture that is dominated by sexual encounters in which authentic intimacy between partners is not a prerequisite or expectation. Often sex is portrayed as a casual tumble in the bed between people who are not necessarily in any ongoing, emotional relationship. One man in our study put it this way: "What is our greatest teacher now? It's TV. They just walk in the door and the next thing they're in bed, and then it's over, and they're on to the next one!"

Of course, it is not only the television that "teaches" people about sex today. Unfortunately, we are bombarded with distorted sexual images—in advertisements, shows, movies, video games, and pornography—on all sorts of electronic devices, from computers to tablets to phones, whether we are purposefully looking for those images or not. Sociologist Michael Kimmel notes that many times those sexualized images are heavily gendered, even violent.[10] As the pornography industry thrives in our country, porn is becoming progressively mainstream, and, sadly, children are exposed to it at increasingly younger ages.[11] Clinical psychologist Catherine Steiner-Adair states forthrightly that "many boys by fourth grade have viewed pornography and their involvement with it tends to grow as they enter preadolescence and adolescence."[12] Both Steiner-Adair and Kimmel note that for a good number of young people, boys in particular, sex education comes via the internet, often via pornography, "however distorted that image of sex may be."[13] Kimmel rightly argues that this form of sex education is "all body and no soul."[14]

Kimmel's research shows that the traditional dating patterns that once dominated our culture have faded. No longer is it the norm to date in order to establish an intimate, emotional relationship/commitment, only *after* which sexual intimacy may occur. Sheila Pickard, who wed Brian fifty years ago, reminded us of those more traditional times. During our interview, she looked at Brian and said, "When we got married . . . your mom said to my mom, 'Do you think they'll know how to do it?'"

The expectations were, of course, that sex was saved for marriage and that two Catholic young people would be clueless about sex, even after an extended period of dating. Sheila expressed regret that back then "Catholics did not talk about sex," so she and Brian were left to figure things out on their own. Ironically, fifty years later, we wonder if people are any better off in "knowing how to do it," or at least knowing how to do it *well*, considering that what they see in their wider environment is mostly: (a) sex that is void of real intimacy and (b) erotic power that is misused, especially "in a culture in which inequalities of race, gender, and class are eroticized" so that "one person's power becomes the cause of another person's pain and humiliation."[15] Sex may be everywhere, but—as Lisa noted above—too often "it's dirty."

Kimmel explains that the old dating patterns, modeled by the Pickards, have been largely replaced in our culture by "hookups," casual sexual encounters that may or may not turn into emotional and/or ongoing relationships. Within this hookup culture, people typically meet at parties or bars and engage in sexual encounters ranging from kissing to sexual intercourse, without any expectation of emotional intimacy (real-life examples of "They just walk in the door and the next thing they're in bed, and then it's over, and they're on to the next one!"). Not surprisingly, Kimmel argues that the sex that is typical in hookup culture *does not prepare people well* for monogamous, healthy, adult sexual relationships in which partners are respected as equals; fidelity exists, allowing partners to be vulnerable to one another; and the sexual needs of both partners are met. Thus, hookups are far from ideal.[16]

C. S. Lewis writes: "Sexual desire, without *eros*, wants *it*, the *thing in itself*; *eros* wants the Beloved . . . *eros* is concerned about the other. One might want 'a man' out of desire for pleasure, but *eros* wants '*this* man'—the person him or herself is desired, not the pleasure he or she can give."[17] Here Lewis reminds us that while sex is often—and ideally—pleasurable, sex at its best is not simply the use of another person as a thing for one's own pleasure, as is the case in pornography and many hookups. Rather, as an expression of erotic love, sex is *personal* insofar as it is unification with a particular beloved, whose flourishing one desires and supports. The Catholic tradition contends that marriage provides an ideal and ongoing context for this kind of sex. It argues that marriage is a relationship in which sex can be "healthy and wonderful," even holy.

Despite this, in our written surveys, only 32 percent of respondents indicate that they *often* or *very often* experience sex with their spouse as "holy" and 29 percent indicate that they *never* experience sex with their spouse as holy. We found this curious and somewhat surprising, and therefore asked some couples that we interviewed to help us understand why it might be that 29 percent of respondents *never* experience sex with their partner as holy. Some suggested that the responses are indicative of what Beth Johnson identifies above: that people may have difficulty thinking of holiness as connected to sex because our culture so often presents sex as void of a spiritual dimension.

Bob Mitchell suggested that people typically associate the word holy with "nuns, priests, and saints" but not with married persons, and even less so with sex. His wife Jeanne nodded her head and said, "In general, talking about holiness is unusual . . . the concept of holiness seems to be unusual and undiscerned. If we take that to the next level and talk about the holiness of sexuality when the messages and images [in our culture are distorted] . . . it seems there is so little that is sacred anymore, much less sexuality. Even though, in the context of twenty-three years of marriage [our sexual encounters] are clearly some of the most sacred experiences that

we have together, there's no language or context for that in our culture."
Bob added: "I don't know that I have ever heard anyone talk about their
sex lives using the language of holiness. Having said that, I think sexual
activity at its finest *is* that."

Perhaps couples could more easily relate words such as *sacred* or *spiritual* (rather than *holy*) to their sexual relationship, if they think of sex as
connected to God at all. Such terms likewise identify that an active sexual
relationship can be a profound way to experience God's grace and goodness
in the married life. Theologian Richard Gaillardetz offers helpful language
for describing what might be called the "holiness" of sex within marriage:

> It is not that . . . lovemaking is some privileged source of grace
> distinct from the many other forms of marital interaction. Mar-
> ried couples abide in God's love, whatever the circumstance, when
> they attend to each other in selfless devotion, placing the other's
> concerns before their own. But there is a sense in which a couple's
> lovemaking ritualizes, as it were, the grace of their daily commu-
> nion with each other. Just as the sacrament of reconciliation as
> celebrated within Roman Catholicism, for example, renders visible
> and effective that divine forgiveness that is always available to those
> who seek it, so marital lovemaking expresses or enacts in a partic-
> ularly explicit way the grace of marital intimacy the couple shares
> in their myriad daily encounters with each other.[18]

Sex within marriage, then, is an important way to ritualize the grace of
daily communion and intimacy that is experienced by couples in myriad
ways—recall for example Kyle's appreciation for tender looks and holding
hands as ways to connect. In our written survey, couples confirmed that
marital sex ritualizes spousal intimacy. Forty-eight percent of people indicated that they experience sex as "an expression of intimacy" *very often*
(the most popular choice out of a list of options). In addition, 32 percent
of respondents experience sex as "an expression of intimacy" *often*, and 14
percent *sometimes* experience sex as an expression of intimacy.

Sex is also experienced by couples as affirmation, celebration, renewal,
pleasure, play, and (less often) as an expression of forgiveness. Interestingly,
one woman said that sex is very "healing" in her marriage, which could mean
that sex is an expression of forgiveness but also could mean that their lovemaking is more generally comforting or reassuring in the midst of stress or
brokenness (perhaps both). It seems that marital sex strengthens and enriches
the spousal relationship, and also functions to build up each of the partners.

In chapter 1, we discussed the importance of married friends delighting in one another, building each other up, renewing one another in difficulty, and meeting each other's needs. In light of our research, it is clear that sexual activity in marriage can function in all of these ways to deepen communion. Over the course of a marriage, the sexual relationship serves as a reminder to each partner: "I love you just because you are you, I delight in your presence, you are precious beyond all saying to me," and therefore I want to be one with you.[19] Surely, this is a grace.

Generativity and Procreativity: About More Than Us

"First comes love, then comes marriage, then comes the baby in the baby carriage." We are likely familiar with this chant from childhood that links marriage to parenthood and thus reflects an institutional model of marriage (more to say about that below). We are also probably familiar with Catholic magisterial teaching (that is, official church teaching coming from the pope and the bishops) that likewise tightly links marriage and procreation. In fact, an openness to procreation is considered by the magisterium to be an essential component to marriage broadly, and to each act of sexual intercourse specifically.[20]

Magisterial teaching thereby emphasizes two inseparable moral meanings of the act of sexual intercourse (and more broadly of marriage): that it expresses and deepens the couple's love (unitive) and that it is open to new life (procreative).[21] Much has been written about how this teaching has been received by Catholics in the United States as well as by members of the Catholic theological community, particularly those who view the teaching through a feminist lens.[22] It is not our intent to directly engage this conversation here, though it is an important one. What we would like to do is emphasize generativity as fundamental to a Catholic understanding of marriage and address the life-giving testimony heard from couples in our study who do not have children; examine some key reasons why the Catholic tradition upholds the goodness of procreation in marriage, weaving in testimony from couples in our study; and highlight some insights about parenting and the married relationship, drawing on sociological data, theology, and the experiences of couples in our project.

Generativity as Fundamental to Catholic Marriage

As we have already noted, from a Catholic perspective, marriage is not meant *only* to serve the good of married partners. In other words, marriage is not merely a commitment that honors and nurtures the love between two married spouses (related to the unitive meaning of marriage), thereby contributing to their good. Instead, the love of the two ought to overflow and extend outward for the good of others and the wider world. Recall Kelly Brown's insight about her marriage in chapter 1, that emphasizes this very point: "It is about us, but has been about more than us . . . the ultimate end [of the marriage] . . . is to bring more God into the world." Following Catholic teaching, Kelly affirms that, ultimately, marriage is about contributing to a common good, or "sharing in the creative purposes of God."[23]

For fertile couples, "sharing in the creative purposes of God" often means the creation of new life through childbearing and/or the nurture and education of life in parenting. But "the generativity [or life-giving aspect] of marriage is *also* realized in the married couple's call to mission, to expansive community."[24] Therefore, "Catholicism's traditional focus on *procreation* in marriage might be broadened profitably" by uplifting and emphasizing a wider notion of marital *generativity*.[25] This move would be particularly meaningful for couples who do not have children, for example, couples beyond childbearing years or those who struggle with infertility. After all, we know well that not every marriage is followed by the baby in the baby carriage.[26] Gaillardetz compassionately acknowledges that "the Catholic Church's strong emphasis on the obligation to have children has left many infertile couples feeling as if they were defective, second-class participants in the sacrament of matrimony."[27]

Indeed, one of us recalls a conversation with a good friend who struggled for many years with infertility before having three children, two of whom are out of college. With pain still apparent in her voice, the friend recalled that in the early years of her Catholic marriage she felt as if her marriage did not somehow meet the standard—or, more accurately, *she* did not meet the standard—because she and her husband did not have babies.[28] She often felt inadequate and remembers being brought to tears during a liturgical celebration that celebrated mothers and motherhood with no acknowledgment of those in the congregation who may be single, struggling with infertility, or beyond childbearing years.[29]

In recent official documents on marriage, church leaders have tried to attend to the danger of overemphasizing procreation without exhibiting sensitivity to persons without children.[30] It would behoove parish leaders to be deliberately attentive to this experience as well. Celebrating the broader *generativity* within marriage—of which procreation is one important manifestation—would be a step in the right direction.

While the vast majority of the couples in our study have children and thus reflected on procreativity and parenthood during our conversations, we heard powerful testimony from couples without children that illustrate the other-centered, life-giving nature of their married communion. Bob and Jeanne Mitchell were unable to have biological children, and Bob identifies that as a moral challenge, explaining that, "without having children, the temptation is to collapse in on ourselves because there is nothing that demands or requires [our immediate attention, for example] asking us to change a diaper. There's nothing. So that's something to be conscious of . . . and is a challenge for us: how do we go beyond self when we don't necessarily have to? There will be no grandchildren to pull us beyond self, so we have to do something more intentional about it." Indeed, Bob and Jeanne have been intentional about reaching out to care for others, particularly young people. For example, they maintain very close relationships with nieces and nephews; have offered extended stays at their home for young people in trouble; mentor youth, especially young men on the margins; and volunteer regularly, both here and abroad.

Another couple that struggled with infertility made a point of not blaming each other for that burden, and decided to make the best of what felt to them like less-than-ideal circumstances. They have become "advocates" for their nieces and nephews, to whom they feel very close. Through the years, they have hosted exchange students and volunteered extensively in their parish, for example, jointly teaching catechism classes. She reads regularly to kindergarten students, and he raises money for Children's Hospital for kids with cancer. Far from closing in on themselves and making their marriage only about themselves, these couples are living out the good of generativity by nurturing life in myriad ways. With the understanding that procreativity is but one expression (albeit an important one) of a marriage's wider generativity, now let us attend more fully to specific reasons for the emphasis on procreation in the Catholic tradition.

Linking Sex and Procreation: To Create These Lives Is Amazing!

At its best, the Catholic church's emphasis on the procreative dimension of marriage is not simply about certain sexual acts but about the life-giving dimension of a union between two embodied selves whose ultimate goal is to "bring more God into the world." One profound reason for the Catholic emphasis on procreativity within marriage is that it honors "the awesome and holy power of procreation."[31] The U.S. Catholic bishops argue that "procreation is a participation in the ongoing creative activity of God."[32]

"Awesome and holy power," indeed; spouses become cocreators with God in bringing children into the world through the communion of their body-selves. Married partners give themselves fully to one another in the act of sexual intercourse, and this *mutual* self-giving sometimes becomes a *creative* self-giving through conception. The couple thereby mirrors our Trinitarian God, whose love is both eternally giving and creative of new life.[33]

When we asked couples, "What about your marriage brings you joy?," often, without hesitation they replied, "Our children!" Indeed, during our interviews we heard parents refer time and again to the power and gift of procreativity in marriage. For example, Sarah Ruffalo and her husband of nineteen years have two children, ages ten and eleven.[34] Sarah remarked, "I just think that my marriage and my kids are such a gift and they have provided so much joy in my life that I know they are gifts from God. It has just made me feel stronger and more faithful, and the children especially . . . to create these lives is amazing. And there has to be something so much bigger and better than us out there to be able to give us these gifts."

Pete and Sally Mahon, parents of two biological and two adopted children, likewise used the language of "amazement" and referred to God's providence when discussing their children. Sally said:

> If we were childless, we would be a happy couple, but I think our children, I would say, have made us laugh the most, or have given that shiver of excitement the most. And there's a big challenge in it. The test of having children, it never stops. I look at my mother, or Pete's mom, and I think, *they're still praying us through*. But it's the joy of the union—how . . . your love and dedication is manifest in the form of your children, as a family. I don't know that we feel that a lot of times we can take much credit—sometimes you're just like, *that's God's grace right now*, but you do see bits of each other in the way your children are, in how they react, or how they struggle, and I just find that really fun. I think it's amazing.

In this reflection, Sally so beautifully speaks of her marital union with Pete—of their love and dedication being manifest in their children, in the family they have created. She so lovingly describes the wonder of parent-hood that has grown from their married love—the laughter, the excitement, the ongoing responsibility, the challenge, the joy, the amazement, and, ultimately, the *grace*. Sally's words bring life, if you will, to the somewhat sterile sounding description of "the unitive and procreative meanings of the sex act." The Ruffalos and Mahons are but two examples of the great many couples who told us that children, and by extension, grandchildren, are the "great joys" of their lives, received as "gifts from God."

Furthermore, in our conversations, spouses revealed an additional gift that procreation brings: that is, the ability to see an already beloved partner in a new way—as co-parent, and in the role of mother or father—thereby deepening love and admiration for them. Phrases such as "I love that he's such a great Dad" and "I appreciate what a fantastic mother she is" were prolific in our interviews.

We highlighted one fine example of this admiration in chapter 1, when Anne Marie Donlan tearfully described how the love and responsibility that Jim shows as a father inspires her to be a better mother. Brendan Ruffalo also is inspired by his spouse as a mother. He calls his wife Sarah the "best mom," explaining that when they became parents, "Sarah became a person that I wasn't surprised to see, but I am always continually impressed to learn from and watch in her role as a Mom . . . that's something that everyday, including this morning dramatically [Sarah looked at him knowingly and they both laughed], she has impressed me with."

In a similar vein, Phil Rullo praised his wife of fifty-two years as mother and grandmother: "Not only do I love Jane for what she is as a mate, but she is probably one of the finest mothers and grandmothers that I have ever seen. And I—one of our granddaughters lives right across the street, so I can see this, naturally, but she is so beloved by our grandchildren—her children, of course—but her grandchildren. She has just shown so much patience and understanding. It's just amazing. I'm in awe of her as a mother and grandmother." Clearly, parenthood (and grandparenthood) enables a new and deeper appreciation and love for one's spouse—yet another grace of procreation, and not a minor one.

An additional reason that the Catholic tradition emphasizes procreativity in marriage has to do with justice, that is traditionally defined as "giving to the other what he or she is due." The logic of Catholic teaching that connects sex, marriage, and procreation is: doing what is just for children—giving to them what they deserve as vulnerable and precious human beings—involves providing a stable environment in which they are properly nurtured and educated. Ideally, marriage provides a secure context in which to raise children. Catholic teaching links marriage to parenthood in part because being raised by two loving parents in a stable home is an ideal environment for children.[35]

Children, of course, are able to fare well in other kinds of environments, such as single-parent families, but studies show the benefits of stable two-parent households on their development; child well-being can be improved by the stability that marriage provides and the social, ecclesial, and legal supports that accompany it.[36] Theologian Cristina Traina argues, "children created carelessly by parents who are not committed to a household, who do not see their children as divine gifts, and who do not see the raising of them as a holy task will suffer. . . . On a societal level, children who lack the social and legal protections that most societies give to marriage typically suffer economic, social, and political marginalization, as do their mothers."[37]

Christian parents are called then, not only to be deeply invested in the well-being of their own children (and committing to fidelity in marriage is an important way to do that), but also to be invested in other families, particularly those who are disenfranchised and lacking support.[38] Both are a matter of justice.

In part, the tight link between sex, marriage, and procreation/parenthood has been loosened by the increasing influence of "the soul mate model" of marriage in our country. The National Marriage Project is a nonpartisan, nonsectarian, and interdisciplinary initiative located at the University of Virginia. More than a decade ago, the Project "called attention to the growing power of a soul mate model of marriage in which marriage is primarily conceived of as a couple-centered vehicle for the pursuit of individual and mutual fulfillment."[39]

It is a more romantic idea of marriage than the older, institutional model, "which sees marriage not only as an expressive vehicle for the couple, but also as an important source of social support, economic cooperation, and care for themselves and their children."[40] Historically, when the institutional model reigned, romantic love was not a prerequisite for marriage. Nor was the self-actualization of the partners a primary concern. Instead, marriage was a social and economic partnership that often focused on children.

Today, only 41 percent of adults consider parenthood to be very important to a successful marriage, down from 62 percent in 1990, according to a recent Pew study.[41] In the soul mate model, children have effectively been de-centered, with the majority of adults indicating that they are not very important (or are nonessential) to a successful marriage.[42] This stands in stark contrast to magisterial teaching that considers an openness to procreation part of the very definition of marriage.

We would like to briefly reflect on the soul mate model of marriage, arguing that it can threaten a Catholic understanding of marriage. First, if marriage is understood to be primarily about the self-fulfillment and mutual fulfillment of the partners, it may threaten a commitment to children. For instance, "a careful analysis of divorce statistics shows that, beginning around 1975, the presence of children in a marriage has become only a very minor inhibitor of divorce."[43] In other words, the weakening of child centeredness has resulted in spouses feeling less obligated to stay committed to a marriage with children because the purpose of marriage is thought to be fundamentally about the emotional happiness and psychological fulfillment of the married partners, however that may be understood. If one ceases to feel fulfilled, so the thinking goes, the marriage is essentially over, and one is justified in dissolving it. Fidelity to children *as part of the marriage commitment* thereby may be undermined.

Second (and related), a soul mate model of marriage can undermine fidelity to one's spouse insofar as it centers on the emotional happiness or fulfillment of both partners who are "in love." A great many young people in our country hold a very romantic notion of the marriage commitment, exemplified in a 2001 study by the National Marriage Project that found that "the overwhelming majority (94 percent) of never-married singles agree that 'when you marry you want your spouse to be your soul mate, first and foremost.'"[44] There is a real danger in the concept of soul mate, in particular if one claims that God has preordained a soul mate for each person, who is somewhere out there to be found. Theologian Richard Gaillardetz rightly argues that if the notion of finding Mr. or Mrs. Right—or *my soul mate*—becomes a matter of discovering who God has preordained for me, it follows that "if a given relationship fails to live up to expectations, it will not be hard to convince myself that I simply failed to listen to God when I made the original choice of spouse."[45]

Echoing Gaillardetz, Jack Baker—husband of twenty-eight years and father of two—strongly rejects an overly romanticized understanding of soul mate that suggests that, should times get difficult, a spouse can simply determine, "You're not my soul mate. I made a mistake in marrying you. I need to go find the one that God has for me." Forthrightly, Jack states, "That's bullshit. You have to work at it. You *become* soul mates. It's not that God says, 'There's a soul mate for you.' It's when you are able to share that very, very intimate love and caring for each other—that *agape* love—that really makes you grow as soul mates." Reflecting on his own marriage, Jack adds: "And we continue to grow—I'm not the best soul mate. And she isn't either, by the way [laughter] . . . but we're getting better each day." With an apology for his language, Jack calls bullshit a soul mate model that pictures marriage as some God-ordained state of romantic bliss that does not involve the daily work of care that makes love grow throughout one's married life. A soul mate model is not all bad, of course. It is good to recognize a romantic or erotic component to marriage and to consider the flourishing of both spouses as an important goal of marriage. But a soul mate model too easily distances romantic love within marriage from *work* and *choice*.[46]

Parenting and the Married Relationship: A Holy Task

"We feel like our goal on earth as parents is to get our children to heaven, and if you can keep that as your focus, it helps you. It helps shape the decisions that you make, I suppose." In chapter 1, we discussed how married partners in our study used the vocational language of "getting one another to heaven" to speak about the purpose of their marriage.

Here, Sophia Vandenbusch uses this language to describe the responsibility she and her husband have for their three children. Clearly, they understand their parenting as a "holy task," a task to which they are fully committed.[47] Their ultimate goal as parents—getting their children to heaven, or bringing them into union with God both in this life and the next—shapes and focuses daily decisions and behavior related to their children's care and development. Ideally, parents make decisions based on shared values and each child's best interest. This is no small feat considering that choices (large and small) abound, including decisions about childcare and how it will be balanced with work outside the home; children's education and moral formation; behavioral and social expectations of children; the nature and extent of extracurricular involvement when children are school-aged; restrictions on the use of technology; household upkeep and the division of household tasks; and the list goes on.

Negotiating these decisions is complicated and sometimes induces conflict. In our written surveys, 67 percent of respondents indicated that "child-rearing practices" are *sometimes* "a source of conflict" in their marriage, while 12 percent indicate that they *often* or *very often* are. Similarly, 65 percent consider "the demands of parenting" to *sometimes* be a source of conflict, while 15 percent indicate that the demands of parenting are *often* or *very often* a source of conflict.

Despite all of the joy and amazement associated with parenting described above, clearly couples also experience conflict as they meet the demands of parenting and raising children. Moreover, 67 percent of respondents indicated that they *at least sometimes* experience "division of household tasks" as a source of conflict, and 73 percent *at least sometimes* experience finding "work/home life balance" as a source of conflict in marriage.[48] We grant that effectively negotiating the division of household tasks and establishing work/home life balance are important tasks for all marriages. The presence of children, however, often intensifies the challenge inherent in these tasks, particularly if both partners work outside the home.

In short, the presence of children—while joyful and wonderful—can strain the married relationship, especially when children are very young, going through adolescence, or have special needs that are temporary or lasting. In light of the strain of parenting and the corresponding possibility of marital breakdown, a 2011 report by the National Marriage Project: *When Baby Makes Three: How Parenthood Makes Life Meaningful and How Marriage Makes Parenthood Bearable*,[49] draws on recent studies in order to identify "aspects of contemporary social life and relationships—from marital generosity to religious faith to shared housework and sexual satisfaction—that seem to boost men and women's odds of successfully combining marriage and parenthood."[50] While here we cannot address each of the identified ten factors that are "associated with higher quality and more stable marriages among married parents in America,"[51] we would like briefly to highlight two of those factors: work and family balance (including shared housework/childcare) and sexual satisfaction.[52]

Parents Finding Work and Family Balance

When Baby Makes Three notes that marriage today is deeply affected by the "gender revolution of the last half-century" as well as changing economic realities in our country.[53] No longer, of course, is a woman legally subsumed under her husband as "head and master," and thus required to "obey her husband" in performing domestic duties.[54] Moreover, the once sharp split that existed between private (domestic) and public realms has softened. Philosopher Pauline Kleingeld explains:

> Beginning in the early modern period, a view came to dominate according to which the family was considered a private realm entirely distinct from the outside political, economic and public spheres. This notion of the family played an important role in legitimating women's legally, economically, politically, sexually, and personally inferior status. The family was conceived of as a special sphere of life depending on the total dedication of women, who were said to be suited for the special tasks of domestic life because of their refined sensibilities and their emotional attachment to husband and children—the very qualities that made them unsuited for the harsh world of economics, learning, and politics. This family was

said to operate purely on the basis of love, and to form a harmonious, complementary unity of interests. As a result, according to the dominant view of the time, it was enough for one person to represent this unity in the public sphere. And the husband, with his greater rational powers and control of his feelings, was thought to be the only one suited for this task.[55]

The women's movement did much to undermine this gender ideology, and equality of women in marriage in the United States today is largely assumed, as is the importance of women's participation in the wider social and political world outside the family. Contemporary magisterial teaching affirms that, while the role of motherhood remains important for married women, "women should have access to positions of responsibility which allow them to inspire the policies of nations and to promote innovative solutions to economic and social problems."[56] In other words, women have a crucial role to play in the public realm as well as the private. Therefore, it is right and just to encourage women to utilize their God-given gifts within and outside the home and to create economic and societal structures that allow for such participation.

Since the women's movement in the 1960s in the United States, women have entered the workforce in large numbers. Unfortunately, the ways that childcare and housework are allotted in many households today do not justly accommodate women's increased participation in the public realm or reflect gender equality.[57] Sociological data continues to show that women do about twice as much work around the house as men.[58] In a *New York Times Magazine* article about gender and parenting, Lisa Belkin writes:

> The most recent figures from the University of Wisconsin's National Survey of Families and Households show that the average wife does 31 hours of housework a week while the average husband does 14—a ratio of slightly more than two to one. If you break out couples in which wives stay home and husbands are the sole earners, the number of hours goes up for women, to 38 hours of housework a week, and down a bit for men, to 12, a ratio of more than three to one. That makes sense, because the couple have defined home as one partner's work. But then break out the couples in which both husband and wife have full-time paying jobs. There, the wife does 28 hours of housework and the husband, 16. Just shy of two to one, which makes no sense at all.[59]

But perhaps the most surprising research shows that in married couples in which the wife has a job outside the home but the husband does not, and where you would assume a complete reversal, the wife nevertheless does the majority of the housework.[60] And while the housework ratio is about two to one (whether families are working class, middle class or upper class), "the wife-to-husband ratio for child care in the United States is close to five to one."[61] Again, whether one parent or both work(s) outside the home does not change this inequity much. If the equality of spouses is truly recognized, in Belkin's words, these at-home work discrepancies *make no sense*. Further, we argue they are a violation of justice.

The 2011 State of Our Unions Report, *When Baby Makes Three*, indicates that "both mothers and fathers are less divorce prone and happier when they report that housework (e.g., cleaning, cooking, taking out the garbage) and childcare are 'shared equally.'"[62] Indeed, deep appreciation for a daily, lived-equality and sharing of roles was voiced by many couples in our study. For example, in their fifty-two years of marriage, Phil and Jane Rullo have enjoyed "a very sharing family life, and a very sharing relationship." Jane said, "Phil has been extremely supportive of me in what I wanted to do. And I was a female at the beginning of the women's movement, and I was also raised in a family where my father said I could do anything that he could do. So it was very important to me that I have a mate who could support what I wanted to do. And Phil has always done that." In their home, Jane explains:

> We never looked along the lines of male-female things. That was never our thing. We pretty much looked along the lines of who physically could do the job better and more efficiently in our home because we both worked, so we had to be efficient in our home life and we had to be efficient in our work life. So we looked at who could probably do it the best and sometimes we looked at who liked to do it more. So just to give you a few examples: I have a brown thumb. I do not have a green thumb. Phil is very good at gardening. I could water a houseplant and say "I love you houseplant," and it would die. [Laughter.] And Phil looks at the houseplant and it thrives and grows all over the whole house. Um, Phil has larger hands than I do so he doesn't do the mending or the sewing when we need to do those things.

"I *have* tried!" interjected Phil, laughing.

Jane continued: "We both cook. In fact our daughters would come home from school, and they would not know who made the cake. They would have to say, 'Dad, did you make this cake, or Mom, did you make this cake?' Phil always does the investing. I always take care of the taxes. I had a little more experience with taxes than Phil did and he had an aptitude for investing. So it kind of came naturally to do what we wanted to do."

Admittedly, not all household tasks are easily or naturally claimed by one partner—for example, Jane said neither of them has a burning desire to take out the trash—in which case, one person does it as an act of service.[63] Moreover, when most efficient, Phil and Jane complete tasks together—like washing dishes and cleaning the house—rather than assuming that the job somehow "belongs" to one or the other spouse. These concrete examples illustrate how the Rullos have successfully divided labor according to talent, interest, and efficiency rather than along the lines of traditional gender expectations.

Phil believes this willingness to share tasks is the result of his upbringing on a farm: "Mom would go into the barn and milk cows; Dad would make bread. Everyone just did a task that needed to be done. No one argued about it—for sure the kids didn't. You did what you had to do. That meant milking cows at five in the morning before school. Anyway, I grew up in an environment where you just did those things and, well, that's carried on in our married life." Jane nodded, adding, "We're both just pitching in as much as we can pitch in."

Dan and Roseann Carr, who both work outside the home, are also apt to pitch in where necessary to get the job done. In Dan's words, "We recognize the need, you know, and just act on it." When asked to tell us about something she loves or admires about her husband, Roseann immediately noted the way that they share tasks in their home: "What I love about Dan is there is no 'I just do the laundry' or 'Dan just does the laundry.' There is no 'I just cut the grass' or 'Dan just cuts the grass.' Last night, he came home, made supper, and started doing the dishes. It's not like a 'his job' or 'her job' at our house. . . ."

Another couple in their focus group nodded in agreement, indicating that it is "exactly the same" at their house: "We don't have his role or my role," the wife said. Her husband added, "I do what I like, she does what she likes . . . and we do most things together." Roseann acknowledged practically that she used to do more of the housework when she was home caring for the children, but now that they both have outside jobs, they divide housework more evenly.

These couples illustrate the value of *mutuality*, that is described by theologian Richard Gaillardetz: "Mutuality is manifested in human relationships wherever and whenever both parties recognize and acknowledge the giftedness of the other. This is quite different from the important, yet in itself insufficient, assertion that each spouse be treated as an equal. When we cultivate mutuality in our marriage, we are learning to recognize not only the equality of each partner but also each one's unique giftedness."[64]

Such mutuality is illustrated by the couples above, who divide roles based on the giftedness of each partner and their likes and dislikes rather than assigning tasks based on restrictive ideas about gender. They see parenting and caring for the household as a mutual obligation and therefore pitch in wherever necessary. Gaillardetz argues—and we agree—that "authentic mutuality within marriage seems to exclude the hierarchical view of the marriage relationship often advocated by fundamentalist Christians . . . [because] mutuality involves the acknowledgement of gifts, [whereas] hierarchical notions of the marriage relationships asks one partner, the wife, to suppress some of her gifts in deference to her spouse." Artificially enforcing narrowly defined gender roles that are part and parcel of hierarchical notions of marriage, and touting them as ordained by God, "brings with it serious risks."[65] As Gaillardetz notes, "Too often the result is a dangerous and potentially corrosive inequity in the assignment of family responsibilities."[66]

Of course, suggesting that the division of labor in the home ought to be *just* and that care for the children and household ought to be *shared* does not mean every household must be structured exactly the same way or that work need always be divided 50/50. How roles are determined, and labor divided, will be prudentially determined by each couple, based on the desires and gifts of the partners as well as the needs of family, home, and wider community. This discernment must be done in the spirit of generosity and gift-giving, rather than being marred by a selfishness that undermines spousal and parental love and responsibility.

Anne Marie Donlon told us that the best advice that her mother gave to her when she got married is: "You have to remember that some days you will do 80 percent of the work and he will do 20. It's never going to be 50/50. Don't expect 50/50 every day or you're going to set yourself up for misery from the start. Your hope is that you get somewhere in the middle ground, but she said, 'You're going to be picking up the slack some days more than he will.' And [that kind of give and take is important] within different areas in your marriage and different times in your marriage."[67]

Affirming this good advice from Anne Marie's mother, we heard time and again from couples that marriage is not a 50/50 endeavor, but instead requires 100 percent effort from each partner. When discussing the importance of mutuality in marriage, Gaillardetz notes that "[n]othing kills a marriage like that deadly game of marital accounting where each keeps track of the 'things done for the other' with the never quite spoken expectation of reciprocation."[68]

Sexual Satisfaction and Parenting

In addition to creating a just work/life family balance, *When Baby Makes Three* also indicates that "married fathers and mothers who report above-average levels of sexual satisfaction are significantly less likely to report being prone to divorce and significantly more happy in their marriages."[69] Yet, as any parent knows, having children can interfere with an active sex life. "After a baby comes along, most couples see their sexual activity and satisfaction drop, at least for a time."[70] Beyond a woman's bodily recovery from childbirth that requires her to refrain from sexual activity, parental care for babies is full-time, exhausting work. And, though the demands of childcare ease somewhat after the first few months of sleepless nights and seemingly constant feedings, raising children nevertheless decreases the time, energy, and privacy available for the marital sexual relationship in an ongoing way.

Of course, marital sexual activity not only is affected by responsibilities directly related to children but by the many commitments and changing circumstances of the lives of married parents. We are pulled in seemingly a million different directions in the course of our days, and sometimes fall into bed exhausted, with little to no energy to spare for our partner. As we know, we are limited body-selves. C. S. Lewis insightfully writes: "I can hardly help regarding it as one of God's little jokes that a passion so soaring, so apparently transcendent as *eros*, should . . . be linked in incongruous symbiosis with a bodily appetite which, like any other appetite, tactlessly reveals its connections with such mundane factors as weather, health, diet, circulation and digestion."[71]

We may not feel like lovemaking because we are not feeling well, or are brutally tired from attending to children, work, or other responsibilities. We may not feel like lovemaking because we are emotionally or mentally distracted at the end of the day—mulling over a situation at work, or worrying about a sick loved one or any number of other matters we may fret about.

Sometimes married partners *do* make love despite not "being in the mood." In our written surveys, for instance, 48 percent of respondents admitted that they *sometimes* experience sex with their spouse as "obligation," while 8 percent experience sex as obligation *often* or *very often*. Keep in mind that these married couples also report regularly experiencing sex as an expression of intimacy, affirmation, celebration, renewal, play, pleasure (all arguably more positive reasons for lovemaking!). Still, it seems important to note that the majority of spouses at least sometimes have sex with their partner out of obligation, presumably because their spouses desire it (only 7 percent claim to *never* experience sex as obligation).

Interestingly, we did not see this break down in any significant way along gender lines—meaning men and women alike feel obliged at times to have sex for the sake of their partner. Rather than viewing this data in a negative light, we interpret it as honest and human, even positive insofar as spouses are generous enough to meet their partner's sexual needs even on occasions when they may not feel much desire. It reminds us of what one man in our study said about married sex: that is, there is no way it can be perfect all the time. The sky "does not always open up and fill with rainbows" when spouses make love. Sex cannot always be perfect because "you bring yourself where you are at that moment," and—as C. S. Lewis notes—at each moment we are captive to our very imperfect, embodied humanity.

All in all, married parents must be on guard to protect their sexual relationship, for the many reasons listed above. We must attentively and actively nurture our sex lives because, as noted, "Sex serves a very serious function in maintaining both the quality and stability of the relationship, replenishing emotional reserves and strengthening the marital bond."[72] Nurturing our sex lives requires that we refuse to let the many pressures that we face prohibit us from connecting sexually. When we sense that our sexual connection is fading for whatever reason, we ought to renew it insofar as possible. *When Baby Makes Three* indicates that "sexual satisfaction is more likely to emerge for women and men in marriages marked by high levels of generosity, commitment, religious faith, and couple-centered quality time. Moreover, women are more likely to report that they are sexually satisfied when they report that they share housework with their husbands. What happens outside the bedroom seems to matter a great deal in predicting how happy husbands and wives are with what happens in the bedroom."[73]

Clearly, sexual satisfaction is tied to the overall quality of the relationship. Clare Bender, who raised seven children with her husband of fifty-seven years, offers some wisdom in this regard:

> [Sex] is just one dimension of a marriage, of a relationship. It is not the most important, it's not the least important. It's important because they're all important. If you want to have a healthy marriage, there are all these different parts that all have to be healthy. They all have to be good. You have to respect each other. You have to have a healthy sexual relationship. You have to have a good faith

relationship together and have to respect each other's families. If there is any one of those parts that's missing or weak, it just weakens your marriage, and the sexual part is just one part like that. You don't look at that alone.

When and how often couples have sex will depend on desire, age, stage of life, and circumstance. Kevin Landwehr movingly talked about how his sex life with his wife has changed over the years: it was once very intense and "kind of held everything together," but as they have matured, while it is less intense, it is still important. He, like Clare Bender, describes the marital sexual relationship as just one part of what binds him and his wife today. Ed Rorholm, whose statement about humans being sexual beings begins this chapter, said—in light of his marriage of more than fifty years—"I feel like the sex can always get better. It's hard to understand that as a young person."

Hard to understand, maybe, but not surprising if one understands the erotic nature of marriage. As the connection between partners deepens over the years—the result of the shared joys and struggles of daily living—it is no wonder that the sex can get better too.

Love Transfigured

Experiencing Sacrament in Daily Living

Matthew Murphy admits that he does not often use the word "sacrament" to talk about his married and family life. It seems too abstract, too theological. Yet, when Matthew tells us about life experiences through which "God becomes real," it is the language of sacrament to which he turns:

> I think with sacrament, it is the opportunity to experience God in a real way. Marriage is an experience of God in a real way with lots of things. It's awe. I remember the first time that I told Margaret that I loved her, and where I was standing. And I remember my knees buckled. Yeah, my knees buckled because I had used that word before in other relationships but there is something different about this. So . . . when you talk about God being awe, or awesome, I can relate to that. Or when you see the crown of your kid's hair coming out in birth and just weeping! That's your first child. Or different aspects of healing with your spouse. . . . We pour out things we might not pour out to another human being: that's sacrament. Now I can understand a little bit about what it means to experience God when I talk about the sacramental. Otherwise I get hung up on the theological language . . . then you lose me real quick.

While Matthew is hesitant to use the theological language of sacrament, his reflections illustrate how he encounters God "in a real way," in the lived reality of ordinary family life, that is precisely the role of sacraments in our lives. Renowned theologian Richard P. McBrien, in describing the sacramental principle, states, "Everything is, in principle, capable of embodying and communicating the divine."[1] Though Matthew claims to get "hung up" on sacramental language, he presents here a strong theological claim: that our lived experiences—such as feeling gratitude and awe before a loved one, seeing the miracle of childbirth, and being courageously vulnerable with one's spouse and thereby experiencing healing—are ways of encountering God.

Angie Smith has been married to Jerry for nearly forty years. They raised eight children and are proud grandparents happy to talk about the delight they take in their many grandkids. Angie reflects on experiencing God in her marriage which, "keeps being something new and something more. . . . God becomes more and more real to us, too, through each other, through these experiences."

Donna Erikson, married to Tim for over three decades, with two sons who have left the nest, also experiences God in her marriage relationship, "God shows His love for Tim through me and His love for me through Tim. And if we keep that going, it's just . . . a whole bunch of love! There is plenty of it!"

Sacraments are the moments large and small in which we glimpse the depth of God's love. Theologian Michael Himes writes: "By 'sacrament' I mean any person, place, thing or event, any sight, sound, taste, touch, or smell that causes us to notice the love which supports all that exists, that undergirds your being and mine and the being of everything about us. How many sacraments are there? The number is virtually infinite, as many as there are things in the universe. . . . For all of you who are married, I hope that one of the deepest, richest, most profound experiences of the fundamental love which undergirds your being is your spouse."[2]

That God's abundant love is experienced in the marriages and families of those we met is no surprise. Theologian Susan A. Ross writes: "According to the sacramental principle, human beings find God not by leaving or denying the world, but by becoming immersed more deeply in it. This is not to say that God and the world are identical, but that God cannot be approached except *through* the world."[3]

Ross's words are echoed in the sentiment of one husband we interviewed who had considered becoming a monk prior to meeting his wife. He recognizes that his spirituality in marriage is not about a life apart but about seeing God in "the ordinary ups and downs of life."

In this chapter we will explore the ways that marriage and family life provide a fruitful context for encountering God. We begin with our couples' explicit descriptions of the presence of God in their marriages, and then probe the ways that such awareness is sustained and shared, namely the importance of ritual, the place of prayer, and the centrality of table fellowship. Building on this exploration of the daily sacraments experienced in marriage, we will look at the importance of marriage as one of the seven sacraments in the Roman Catholic tradition.

A Place of Holy Encounter: God Just Comes Along

Referencing the Vatican II document *Gaudium et Spes* (the Pastoral Constitution on the Church in the Modern World), the U.S. bishops instruct, "Marriage signifies and makes present to baptized spouses the love of Christ by which he formed the Church as his spouse: 'just as of old God encountered his people in a covenant of love and fidelity, so our Savior, the spouse of the church, now encounters Christian spouses through the sacrament of marriage.'"[4]

This might sound like language reserved for church declarations, but time and again the couples we encountered spoke in terms such as these. Margaret Murphy explains: "If I think of God's love for me, probably the biggest way it's been shown is through Matthew's love for me. And I have always felt loved. . . ."

Matthew's love for Margaret uncovers what theologian Bernard Cooke calls God's self-revelation: "In our love and concern for one another, in our friendships and in the human community that results, we can gain some insight into what 'God being for us' really means."[5]

That type of ever-present love, even love beyond what one may feel is deserved, is echoed in the words of Bob and Jeanne Mitchell, who have learned about unconditional love, for one another and for others, in the context of married life. Jeanne explains, "[It's about] more than we have. More than someone deserves. More than having to earn it—the abundance." Bob nods in agreement, adding, "[We] embrace the idea of love that is undeserved—unconditional love." He goes on to explain that what is central in this perspective is giving: one gives unconditional love without thought of return.

Kevin Landwehr, married to Lisa for over forty years and the father of five, reflected on the abiding presence of his wife through good days and bad as a place of encounter with God: "When you love somebody as much as I love Lisa, God just comes along."

Phil Rullo, speaking from the wisdom of more than five decades of marriage, reflected on the way that marriage has brought him closer to God: "And if you have love, if you have patience, if you show understanding and gentleness—and there is plenty of that in our relationship—all of those things are Christ-like and God-like. All of those things bring us closer to God."

Indeed, it is the daily practice of these virtues that draws couples into deeper connection with God. As theologian Richard R. Gaillardetz describes, "The spiritual challenge of our lives lies not in desperately setting aside moments for God alongside the other activities and commitments of our lives, but rather that of discovering *within* our basic human activities and commitments the possibility for communion with God. . . ."[6] We are invited daily to open our eyes to the presence of God, not despite the complex and often busy lives we have as couples and families, but *through* the relationships and commitments that mark our days.

These deep encounters with the generous love of a spouse allowed our couples to consider marriage as a sacramental experience. Bill McCarthy understands the sacramental nature more deeply today, now that he and Katie have raised their kids and sent the youngest off to college; he says, "I don't think for myself I understood the sacrament of marriage fully probably until the last fifteen years. Just having the kids I realized the blessings that came from our commitment to each other. And to feel the love I feel from my wife, to think that the Lord loves us even more is just ah!—that's pretty cool."

Other couples describe the "grace and beauty" they see in their marriage sacrament, or refer to their marriage vows in terms such as "sanctity . . . gravity . . . profundity." This sanctity is not only about the marriage ceremony entered into on a particular day; it is about the lived and evolving experience of marriage. Joe Johnson sees that: "The sacraments are verbs, not nouns. They are what we do. Marriage isn't something that you go through one day and that's it. You're living it out every day, every minute." It is to this everyday living that we now turn, exploring how that sacramental vision can be fostered and supported in three significant ways: ritual, prayer, and the family table.

The Importance of Ritual: She Could Count on It

The daily routine of a loving husband making his wife's coffee in the morning, or the annual tradition of a mother with a full-time career outside the home who takes off the first and last days of her children's school year so she can be present to them in these transition moments, are just two of the many examples we heard of rituals valued by the couples we encountered.

Todd Phillips, married to his high school sweetheart for over thirty years, reflects on the importance of a family ritual for their daughter, now in her mid-twenties and living over a hundred miles away: "Our daughter, when she was in preschool, she made an angel out of paper plates and at Christmastime, we put it on top of the tree. . . . So we have to wait until our daughter comes home [to put the angel on the tree]. She lives out in [another town] now so we have to wait. It isn't Christmas until she gets home and I put out the stepladder and she gets up there and has to put her angel on the tree." This treasured and reliable ritual is important to the entire family. Todd's wife Jenny explains that the angel has its own box; each year this paper plate creation is packed away with the care one might reserve for a crystal tree-topper.

Another father in the same focus group nodded and shared his perspective on why family rituals such as this are so important: "Your daughter could count on it. It wasn't Christmas until she put that damn thing on the tree. This thing she made so long ago that wasn't worth a nickel to anybody else but is worth everything to your family. She could count on it."

Theologian Maureen Gallagher helps us understand why rituals such as these can be so deeply revered: "[J]ust as the church celebrates sacraments in the community, so does the family ritualize its gifts, its ups and downs, its brokenness, its giftedness. . . . It experiences life every day; at certain times such as birthdays, parties, Sunday dinners or brunches, it takes life in slow motion so its members can come to new realizations, new awareness of what they mean to each other. At such times families take their raw experiences, make them significant, and celebrate them. This is the heart of sacramentality."[7]

And so a simple angel made from paper plates comes to have real meaning because year after year it slows down time and reminds the Phillips family of their deep connectedness, even now that they live in different parts of the state.

To our surprise, when we asked couples about rituals or traditions in their marriages and family life, they often hesitated initially. More often than not they assumed we meant something "churchy" and were not sure they had anything to say. As the interviews continued, couples would naturally allude to a practice we heard as ritual, and we would stop and redirect. "That's what we mean by ritual!" one of us would exclaim. And then we would learn a little more.

We heard about sharing a relaxed cup of coffee on the weekend, a ritual acknowledged as only being possible now that the kids are no longer young and clamoring for early-morning attention. We heard about Saturday evenings when a hardworking couple with dual careers and a hobby farm spent deserved relaxation time listening to *A Prairie Home Companion* while enjoying a glass of wine. We heard about rituals that send off the children so the parents can connect; one couple has taught their children that after dinner Mom and Dad get twenty minutes at the table sans interruption. And we heard about rituals that are built around the children; in one case, a family has a weekly tradition of saying one nice thing about each other. One can only imagine the effort that takes in some moments of family life!

Some couples have very intentional ways of staying connected in the midst of work, schedules, and even struggle. One husband calls his wife each day at noon; one couple sets aside one weekend per month to focus on their relationship and eschews other commitments; another couple told us they have a "secret squeeze"—in times of difficulty, sometimes in moments when they find it difficult to connect in any other way, they gently squeeze their interlocked hands three times as a reminder they are always there for one another. Each of these moments, some even seeming small to the couple describing them, remind the family members of their connection and value. They build up the community of the family.

As Gallagher notes, rituals also serve to mark time. Some rituals are daily, such as a mother who lies down with her daughter each night at bedtime and shares a story of her childhood. Now nearing twelve years old, this daughter still wants to hear these nightly renditions of Mom's "when I was a little girl" stories.[8]

Other rituals are annual demarcations built around a wider circle of family. One woman spoke of an annual back-home campout where her siblings and their families camp in their parents' yard. Aptly nicknamed "Moochfest," this is one time each year when the adult children (and their children) mooch off the hospitality of Mom and Dad! Another couple, Dan and Roseann Carr, has been married thirty-two years. They have happily transitioned into the grandparent stage of family life and seem to act as the elders of their extended families. Dan's family gathers annually for his Dad's birthday, celebrating by shooting trap and sharing a potluck supper. Roseann's extended family commemorates the anniversary of her mother's death: "That is the one thing that all my kids and all my brothers and their kids [do], we all go to church together. It's like a given. That's our one thing, whatever Sunday is closest . . . and then we do a big meal together."

Whether the reliability of a consistent bedtime ritual or annual gatherings that are understood by all as given, family rituals move with a rhythm the members understand and value. Like the seasons of a church year, these rituals mark important times in the life of the family.

While only mentioned by a small number of those we interviewed, we were moved by the example of those who routinely declare in writing the importance of those they love. One husband makes a silent retreat annually; in the past twenty-seven years he has only missed it four times! Part of his ritual on this retreat is to write a letter to his wife that reflects on their past year together and expresses gratitude for her ongoing presence in his life.

Phil and Jane Rullo enjoy writing and have made it an enduring part of their marriage, now spanning over five decades. Both were invested in active careers, and when either would travel for work he or she would leave notes behind for the spouse at home, or send off the traveling spouse with notes stuck in the luggage—one note for each day apart. Jane described how Phil's work often took them away for New Year's. When the children were young, they were watched by their grandparents, but Jane wanted the children to hear from her the first day of a new year. "So I started writing them Happy New Year letters—notes that they now actually have a little pile of. And my mother would read the notes to them because they got the notes before they could read."

These days, Phil writes an annual letter to each family member as well— not only his children but his children's spouses and their grandchildren. Jane continues, "It's a letter telling them how you felt about the year with them and everybody looks forward to that. . . . We still continue to write those letters."

Not all families are filled with writers, but we imagine the treasured canon of a pile of letters marking time by expressing what the past year held and what each family member means to the writer. Some families write an annual Christmas letter or keep a journal in a family cottage to note who has visited—these too are ways of ritualizing in words the connection the family experiences, the community they are.

Rituals are attempted, tested, adapted. And some just do not work! Jim and Anne Marie Donlan had the focus group in stitches as they described a Lenten practice undertaken in earnest. Jim had been raised by a mother who emphasized Lenten practices as both giving up and doing something more. So one year he decided he could do something more by preparing a hot breakfast for the family each morning of Lent. Jim is a morning person so did not mind the sacrifice of waking early to prepare the pancakes or omelets and bacon. But teenage children are more inclined to granola bars grabbed on the way out the door, allowing for as many minutes of sleep as possible. Anne Marie foreshadowed for us, "This required the children to get up a little earlier to eat. . . ." Jim admitted, "Oh, they didn't want to!" Anne Marie reminded Jim he could have changed it; they did not have to endure resentful, angry breakfasts for forty days. But Jim would hear nothing of turning back on his commitment. Anne Marie summarized her take-away from Jim's Lenten generosity that met with high school hostility:

"That was *my* desert!" Jim shook his head and smiled, "Well, that was a ritual we tried. . . . We laugh about it now. . . ."

As couples and families work to establish meaningful rituals, they do well to carry some of this lightness of heart to the work. Some family rituals are designed, intentional, and successful. Others we stumble into, adapt or eventually admit, "Oh well, we tried!" But couples and families are enriched by rituals that remind them of the seasons of their lives and the value they find in one another.

Some rituals in which couples engaged had clear religious connections. One family created a candle with their children, painting on it various images and symbols. When someone in the family became aware of a person needing prayer, the family would light the candle and pray together for that intention. Another couple blesses their children each morning as they leave the house. In an era when school shootings appear in the news on an all-too-regular basis, it is easy to understand the comfort, for parents and kids alike, of a daily ritual of blessing.

Jack and Gretchen Baker described a beautiful bedtime ritual: When their children were young, Gretchen would read them bedtime stories as so many families do. What made this ritual distinct was that she would alternate between reading her sons a story and praying a decade of the rosary with them. And so the young boys grew to rely on a nighttime litany of prayer, storybook, prayer, storybook. Gretchen was raised in a family that enjoyed the devotion of praying the rosary, but Jack was not. He knew about this ritual, but for a long while he held back, embarrassed that he did not know how to join in. He describes how he eventually entered into this family ritual:

> She finally sent the boys out, "Dad, you want to pray? You want to come in, we're gonna pray the rosary?" So my boys were inviting me, okay. And it came a day, or a night, when they came out and for a couple nights before that, I thought, *I don't know how to pray the rosary*. And I said that to my youngest—he would have been six, seven at that time or whatever—but he responded, "That's okay, we can teach you." So I remember going in there that night and sitting underneath their window, kind of curled up, and them saying the rosary, but I didn't—I knew the Our Father and obviously everything else—but I didn't know the mysteries or the ending prayers. And yet they did. And so it wasn't the first night, but it's one of the nights after that I'm lying there and I'm thinking, "Oh my goodness, my boys are teaching me how to pray." So we prayed the rosary after that almost every night for years as part of going to bed.

"Almost every night for years." This is a clear marker of a ritual that has an established place of importance for a couple or a family. We met one parent who joked that anything the kids enjoy they like to declare a tradition! But significant rituals have sustained seasons of importance. The couples we interviewed indicated their family rituals sometimes shifted over time, but those of importance—whether they are nightly or annual or somewhere in-between—occur reliably and become important cornerstones for a life shared in common.

The Place of Prayer: It's Not All About You

As seen in the above example of the Baker family who shared story time interspersed with decades of the rosary, prayer is an important ritual to the couples we encountered. We were impressed, and often humbled, by the rich prayer lives of the couples we met.

As noted in chapter 1, Pete and Sally Mahon decided early on that the Prayer of St. Francis held deep meaning for them. So they committed to praying it together each night of their marriage. Sally describes their practice: "There are very few nights we don't say it. . . . And it's hard to say when you're mad at each other! But sometimes, one of us would go, 'We should say our prayer,' and you can't not say it then!" One can only imagine what it is like to recite together "Let me seek not so much to be consoled as to console . . . to be understood as to understand" in the midst of an argument! Especially in moments of difficulty, this prayer ritual beckons the Mahons to greater love and forgiveness.

Another couple mentioned sharing nightly prayer over the phone during an era when the husband traveled frequently for work. One couple described their routine of praying for the future spouses of their still-young children, asking God to bless them with safety and goodness. One woman described her daily prayers for the members of her extended family, both those related to her and those from her husband's side of the family: "Having them in my life is a constant prayer reminder, if you want to call it that, that these people are special in my life and I really need to keep them in prayer or thank God for them every single day."

Bob and Jeanne Mitchell, married for over twenty years and a couple for more than three decades, are an active and outdoorsy pair. Bob describes the way they experience prayer in nature: "The times that we are together, we can slow down and paddle a canoe, there's a certain rhythm that goes with it, there is a meditative quality about that." Jeanne nods and recalls hearing somewhere that stained glass windows in churches were created to mimic sunlight filtering through dense forest trees. "I think about that now, both in church and when we are in the woods," she says. Whether describing a traditional devotional prayer such as the rosary, or the attentiveness to the beauty of God's creation, our couples spoke eloquently about moments of prayer in their marriages and family life.

Many couples we met told us, almost apologetically, about practices of prayer before meals. They would often convey—with a shrug that perhaps revealed they were not sure if what they were about to say really *counts*—that one of the ways that their family routinely prays together is by saying grace.

Theologian L. Shannon Jung asserts that this daily prayer ritual matters a great deal. Jung describes three important aspects of a simple table blessing: praising God, blessing the food —an act of returning it to God, its source— and giving thanks.[9] From Jung's vantage point, our couples need not have been timid in describing table prayers as one of their ongoing practices: "Saying grace is terrifically important for children. Most significantly, being formed in gratitude as a response to grace may be the foundation of living faithfully and joyously."[10]

Clearly, prayer is important to the couples with whom we spoke. Of the couples we surveyed, 70 percent indicated shared prayer is an extremely important way to encourage faith in their homes. Though they affirmed the importance of prayer in principle, some couples helped us see the nuances in living out a committed life of prayer together. One woman described the different prayer styles she and her husband prefer: "I love being at retreats. . . . I love being in nature; he loves to pray the rosary . . . we are on totally different pages and that is okay." Another couple acknowledged, "Since retirement, we have more time to pray. And we have more time to pray together and I really think that's important."

These couples' experiences are in line with the insights of Gaillardetz, who notes both the challenges of finding time for prayer in the busyness of family life and the distinct prayer styles and preferences each partner may bring to the marriage. He cautions against viewing prayer as the most important measure of marital spirituality, reminding the reader that God does not *become* present in prayer. Rather, our prayer lives can help "cultivate a heightened appreciation of the God who is always present to us."[11]

Understanding variations in prayer styles and the time available for prayer at different moments in married life, it was clear that sharing prayer held a place of deep importance for many couples we met. The Browns, married nearly twenty years and raising three grade school children, described the surprise and importance of praying together within the first twenty-four hours of meeting. Kelly noted it "was a big tip-off to us that we actually prayed together out loud." They both acknowledged that they had never done that. Kelly continued, "And that was significant to us. It kind of tipped us off to the significance of our relationship and the significance of who we could be together."

Ted and Paula Peterson, married over fifty years, also prayed together before they were married. Paula told us how important she thought it was for their children to catch them in the act —of prayer! "It binds the family when they come in to say an extra goodnight and see mom and dad kneeling there; it just means so much."

Joycelyn and Randall King married later in life and never had children. The two share a deep spiritual connection and commitment to regular prayer. As Joycelyn says, "One thing that brings me really profound joy is that Randall and I share a deep spirituality." She went on to describe their moments of shared prayer as "very grace filled," and she smiled as she acknowledged that these moments "bring joy."

Another couple described the way the challenges of adoption strengthened their prayer life as a couple: "It just seemed like a natural inclination, you know, let's pray about this. Then it's not all about you."

Perhaps this act of praying together felt natural because turning to prayer in a situation of need is a common experience. Many people first encounter these moments of pleading with God in middle school when facing a test for which they are inadequately prepared! But our couples faced more difficult challenges, such as infertility, unemployment, or the stress of a home addition compounded exponentially by a problem that could take the house.

Marge and Randy Peterson were devastated when the opportunity to expand their home for their growing family nearly caused them to lose it. They look back on this not as a struggle but as a time for deep prayer, shared prayer, family prayer. Marge describes the experience: "We tried to add an addition to our home, and when the contractors were digging, they found seventy-five gallons a minute of water coming out of the hole that they had dug for us!" Stunned and concerned, Marge asked the family to go to church with her; she felt a deep need to pray: "We went straight over there and I do a daily devotional book and that day the Psalm was: 'I am drowning in the waters. . . .' And I almost cried. I almost cried."

We learned that Randy and Marge do not share all the same prayer preferences: he praises God singing in the church choir and she prefers to read enriching devotionals or sit in silence in front of the Blessed

Sacrament. But in this time of stress, we see Randy's willingness to join with his wife, and together with their children, in a form of prayer Marge finds deeply consoling. She recalls, "That was probably the most we have prayed together. We prayed our separate ways, too, but we prayed together a lot." Eventually the contractors solved the issue, but at that moment when they were indeed "drowning in the waters," it was in the act of shared prayer that Marge and Randy knew they were not alone.

Among the rich prayer experiences shared by our couples are experiences in their faith communities, including engagement with the sacraments of the church. Pete and Sally Mahon explained how important it is to them to attend Mass on a regular basis, both individually and together, seeing it as a place they "check in" with God. Clearly they understand this experience of checking in as one that grounds them and helps them live as they are attempting to. Sally hinted at this, referring to the regular practice of attending Mass as a needed "course correction." She went on to explain that when she and Pete attend Mass several times a week, "I just know that I am and we are as a couple, too, on our game a little more and have a better compass or something."

Similarly, Jerry and Lisa Simms described weekly Mass attendance as a "reset button." They know what it can be like for families with children to muster the energy, the courage, and the semi-clean socks to get to church! But they see the reward for the effort. Together they painted the scene: "Every Sunday, it can be a bad morning, it can be a good morning, but then we go to church, and it's kind of like a reset button on the day." And Jerry continued, "Yeah, like you recharge. It's a reset. You're starting over, and you might have been disagreeing about, or you're flustered as you're leaving the house and something's not going right or someone's not cooperating or whatever, and you walk in and you're still kind of tense from that situation, and by the end it's okay, now we can start over."

An older couple experiences Mass as a time of great togetherness. They described their decades-long practice of going to communion side-by-side, hand-in-hand. The husband is a convert to Catholicism; his wife walked up the aisle holding his hand the first time he received communion, and they have never stopped. Sometimes fellow parishioners will greet them in the grocery store or around town. They may not know them by name, but they recognize them hand-in-hand and call out, "Hey, I know you!"

Jeremy and Kathleen Cotter are both converts to Roman Catholicism, as mentioned in chapter 1. Kathleen converted first, with Jeremy following years later. They came to Catholicism from a distinct place—having been longtime members of one of the traditional peace-keeping churches and having, for years, raised their children in an intentional Christian community. Jeremy explained how he, a former pastor, eventually followed his wife to their Catholic parish community: "For me it was the Mass and just the beauty and depth of the liturgies, the Mass. And there is—I think—a spirit-led genius in the Catholic church that the centerpiece of the Mass is coming to be fed—it's always coming to be fed and then be sent out."

Feeding and sending are clearly centerpieces of the experience of Mass. But they are also in the fabric of the various rituals couples shared with us. Partners and their families took nourishment from reliable and significant rituals, including prayer experiences, and so fortified were able to carry their faith into the challenges of life both big and small.

As we will explore more fully in our consideration of service and hospitality, these deep roots gave our couples strength to engage compassionately with the world beyond their doorstep. Our exploration of sacrament in daily living demands one additional arena of consideration: the powerful experience of being fed that drew Jeremy Cotter to the Catholic tradition is encountered nowhere more explicitly than at the family table.

The Practice of Table Fellowship: I Wouldn't Change That

Couples with older children have the opportunity to hear their children reflect on the importance of gathering at table, a sometimes challenging and contested aspect of family life. One woman recalled her oldest returning on break from a first year at college. The woman inquired about the aspects of home that her daughter was missing the most. "The only thing she really missed was breakfast," the mother laughed and shook her head. "But I prepared that. I fixed breakfast all throughout high school for everybody. But I was like, really? That's the only thing you missed? Breakfast?" She laughed some more and concluded, "Okay, well, I'll take that, I guess."

After years of trekking children to their various activities, staying up with them through nights of illness or worry, and building rich family traditions, parents may deem breakfast a small matter. But then we imagine that first-year college student missing the comfort of fumbling into the family kitchen with pj's on, eyes barely open, only to be greeted with a "good morning" smile and a plate of food that someone cared enough to prepare for her specifically. Now that young woman is away at college where she has to get dressed and walk across campus, find her ID if she is to be known, and where—even on campuses where the food is prepared with care—it has been made not for her personally but for the collective entity "the students." In light of all the sacrifices a parent makes, breakfast may seem small, but the importance of a place at the table is clearly significant.

Jim and Anne Marie Donlon watched with pride and a bit of concern as their two sons entered the military. The same boys who, when teenagers, would contest family meals, frequently declaring, "Nobody else's parents make their kids come home for dinner!" now see things a bit differently. When one son was home on leave for Mother's Day, he told Anne Marie about a conversation about growing up that he and his brother had in a bar one night when they were stationed in the same place. Clearly moved by the memory, Anne Marie paused to wipe her eyes, and recalled: "We had this great conversation about all these things the kids remember doing and the dinners. He said, 'We used to give you such a hard time about the dinners . . . I wouldn't change that. I didn't realize how many people didn't have that growing up and how important it would be in my life.'"

The appreciation of these grown sons is what parents of younger children need to hold in their sights, even as the toddler is fidgeting, one sibling taunts another, and the teenager rolls her eyes at the family with whom she is stuck dining!

At times, family meals are moments of delight not only in retrospect, but as they are occurring. L. Shannon Jung, reflecting on the connections between Eucharist and the family table, points out, "Eating is a time for delighting not only in the food but also in each other. Eating together can heal old riffs, head off new ones, and build community."[12]

Al and Christine Kozak place importance on family meals with their five young children. In addition to daily meals with as many family members assembled as schedules allow, they put a big focus on an all-family meal at least one night each weekend. Al describes how the many demands of family life can stretch you to the point of breaking if you are not intentional about gathering together. In their family, that gathering is focused around the table: "Our kitchen table is a big place for our family. It's where we come back and we have to have a meal together. You know our Catholic faith and Jesus says, come back to the table. A lot of good discussions have happened at our kitchen table. . . ."

He goes on to name topics as important as marriage and jobs and as mundane as the scheduling for an upcoming day. It is the practice of being together at table that maintains connection by making space for conversations big and small.

Many families ensure that conversation at table draws in all the members. One couple with ten- and eleven-year-old children is deliberate about setting the table and sitting at it together. When the couple realized that merely inquiring about a good or interesting part of the day was often unproductive and yielded little more than shrugs or grunts, they began asking their children to tell a story—a story about a good part of the day, a bad part of the day, even an amusing moment. As their kids relayed *stories*, these attentive parents were able to hear hints of relationship, activities, or moments of import in the lives of the children.

Jerry and Lisa Simms and their three sons are together at table frequently. "And we eat at the table. So that's absolutely, probably one of the biggest rituals and one of the most important rituals in our family—sitting down and eating together as a family." While the Simms family eats, they discuss their days, often asking about best or worst moments of the day but also asking about the funniest moments, or even throwing in random questions, such as, "What flavor of ice cream do you wish you could eat right now?"

Jerry and Lisa's youngest son is on the autism spectrum and became part of their family through adoption when he was four years old. They utilize nightly mealtime conversations as a way to understand the type of day he has had. Jerry described this: "In the beginning, he didn't know what to do with 'What was your good part?' Well, the good part might have sounded like the bad part or it might have all sounded the same. But a lot of times you'll kind of get an idea about how he thinks his day went, 'cause you'll say, 'Bad part?' and he'll just give you a thumbs up, so 'nope, no bad part. I had a good day.' So we kind of get a feel for where he's at emotionally for the day too."

In his book, Jung reminds us, "Sharing one's meal with others is a time-tested way of building community in the church. It is a means of transformation for the people of God."[13] Theologian Julie Hanlon Rubio describes the importance of the family table: "The family meal, like the Eucharist, is important, not because it is the high point of the family's life, but because it symbolizes what the family is and what it does. If the family meal is neglected, not only do the relationships among family members suffer, but so does the sense of what the family is about. The meal brings the family together and provides an opportunity for shared talk, celebration, and mission."[14]

Roseann Carr knew the importance of gathering the family at table, having raised her children with regular experiences of family meals. But now in the role of grandmother and matriarch, and busy with multiple

jobs and community involvements, she had begun to overlook the need
for such gatherings—until her young niece, Abigail, asked her one day:
"'Aunt Roseann, how come we never come to your house anymore? We
always used to come to your house!' So now since January, we have what I
call Abigail Get-togethers. We pick a Sunday once a month that works for us
and whoever can, comes, whether it is ten people or all thirty-eight of us."

Abigail paved the way for Roseann and her husband, Dan, to build community in their wider family by calling the group together to table again,
with a warm welcome to come as you are and when you can. Our church
communities do well when they extend a similar joyful welcome to those
who return to the table to be nourished.

A Sacramental Tradition: They Know They're Loved

Thus far we have considered the ways that our daily lives are the locus
for encountering God, and the ways that family rituals, prayer, and meals
help us to recognize God in our living. In this way we have explored daily
family life as filled with sacramental experiences. But this is not to suggest
that the Roman Catholic understanding of marriage as one of the seven
sacraments is unimportant. To the contrary, we believe it is because the
couples we met are steeped in the rich sacramental tradition of the church
that they are equipped to bring this understanding to daily life.

Our consideration of the sacramental aspect of marriage in the Roman
Catholic tradition would be impoverished if we did not probe more explicitly connections to the church's sacrament of matrimony, a connection recognized and valued by couples in our study. For example, those we surveyed
indicated that they entered into marriage viewing it as a sacrament—93
percent of the couples married in the church indicated that seeing marriage
as a sacrament was "extremely important" in their decision; in fact, it ranked
highest among the various criterion offered in the question.[15] Viewing marriage as a sacrament offers a more hopeful narrative of its possibilities, sets
marriage in the context of community, and offers a framework in which to
view families as domestic churches. We first turn our attention to the need
for a more hopeful narrative of marriage.

A quick search online reveals more than thirty wedding-related "reality" television shows —admittedly a quickly changing landscape but one
with entries including *Bridezillas, Engaged and Underage, Four Weddings*—
in which four brides compete to determine who had the best wedding,
the winner and her new husband winning a luxurious vacation—and, of

course, *Say Yes to the Dress* and its many dress-related spin-offs, all of which build plenty of drama and often infighting into the process of finding the perfect wedding gown. Television producers have hit on a gold mine as they find that these low-production-cost shows have wide appeal. While some programs seem less objectionable than others, what they all share is a disproportionate focus on the wedding ceremony as a spotlight event in which the bride and groom—from the vantage point of the shows, mostly the bride—are stars for the day. It seems clear that the featured Bridezillas (bride + Godzilla = basically a woman who has decided that since she will soon marry she has every right to treat friends, family, businesspersons, and her future spouse as though they were her servants, and failing in their roles!) are not informed by the perspective of the U.S. Catholic bishops who teach that, "As a sacrament, marriage signifies and makes present in the couple Christ's total self-gift of love."[16]

Viewing marriage as sacrament is a hopeful narrative in a landscape where hope is needed. It reminds us that even if the dresses do not zip, the photographer shows up at the wrong church, and the bakery delivery person drops the cake, a beautiful sacrament can emerge from a wedding debacle unharmed. It does not suggest the engaged couple should not care about the details of their wedding day, a day of joy and celebration with those they love most, but it grounds the focus firmly in the sacrament that begins that day and shapes a life together.

As with all sacraments in the Catholic tradition, community is central to the sacrament of marriage. Our couples spoke often about what it meant to take their vows in front of others—to stand surrounded by an assembly and make their vows in the presence of God. As one man explained, "We all stood up on an altar in front of our friends and family and God and everybody." At times a thoughtful priest or deacon will address the congregation at a wedding and remind them of their responsibility to the newly married couple. But the responsibility flows both ways, as we heard from one woman who smiled as she thought of her wedding day and the priest saying, "All these people are here today because they love you and support you. But they are also expecting something of you. And they are going to be watching you." She carries that understanding still, telling us, "Our marriage should be a mirror of love to other people."

This mutuality of the communal experience is something we heard time and again from the couples with whom we met. They looked to their church communities for models of living a faithful life, and they understood they were called to be models for others.

Bill and Katie McCarthy live in a bowling town where lots of couples enjoy regular time together in leagues that are as much about laughter and a frosty mug as they are about bowling the perfect game. Katie laughs as she recalls her altered bowling technique when she was nine months' pregnant with their first child! But she gets more serious as she tells us of a weekly bowling date she and Bill shared with his parents. "I think about that relationship we had with his parents, just the two of us one-on-one with them, which, looking back at it, was awesome. They are good role models," she says. Bill nods as the two recall being mentored in the early days of their marriage by the strong example of his parents.

Not all couples looked up to the marriage of both spouses' parents, but most couples spoke of some model, often a parent, sometimes a sibling or dear friend. The couples we met spoke not only of these immediate models, people with whom they had close relationships, but also of the modeling encountered in the life of an active parish, where you witness stories unfolding week-to-week.

Frank and Kelly Brown have been married nearly twenty years but still see themselves as one of the younger couples in their parish. Frank notes the importance of the others, "Especially for us as a younger couple to have so many examples for us to look to as we grew in our marriage." Another group had an especially rich exchange about the importance of their parish in sustaining family life:

> One woman began: "On Good Friday, when you see people you know go up who can barely kneel down and kiss that cross—that just—you know, you realize the oneness that you are with everybody."

> Another woman added: "Watching these kids from little bitty; and all of the sudden they are off to college and beyond. You look around church again and you see all these families grow. It's very powerful."

> Her husband chimed in: "Your kids come back and they see, especially after Mass, everybody talking. 'Hey, how are you? Hey, haven't seen ya. . . .' That's something that [our older kids] may have questions with their faith, but again, going back to that community; they know when they are there at Christmastime. . . ."

> His wife interrupts: "It's a family. They know they're loved."

> Another man concludes: "You almost want to be at every Mass so you don't miss somebody."

The model of an elderly person venerating the cross, families growing over the years, the experience of a college student or young adult being warmly greeted in what may be a rare appearance inside a church, these are some ways our parish communities hold and enrich married couples as they strive to live faithfully.

Just as others model holiness for them, our couples understood the call to model their faith for others. Margaret Murphy explained, "I also thought right away that our marriage as sacrament also means very strongly that it cannot be, like the light under the bushel, an insular thing, a Matthew and me, a me-and-Jesus kind of thinking, like it's all about me and Jesus. Well, it's not just about Matthew and me. It's not even just about us and our family and what we have. It has to be something more. That's where that sacrament [comes in], the sign of a presence that our life cannot be lived in an insular bubble."

Indeed, Margaret is in agreement with the U.S. bishops in her conviction that the marriage she and Matthew entered into is not about them alone. The bishops write, "The marital vocation is not a private or merely personal affair . . . but it is also for the good of the Church and the entire community. . . . The living-out of marriage takes place within the whole Body of Christ, which it serves and in which it finds nourishment."[17]

It is because our marriages provide the context in which we strive to live out the call to holiness[18]—taking nourishment from and serving the wider community—that the home is looked at as a church within the church.

This church within the church is often called the domestic church. The language of family as domestic church, or *ecclesia domestica*, was brought back into usage with the documents of Vatican II and is explored by the U.S. bishops in their pastoral letter, *Love and Life in the Divine Plan*. The documents describe a locus of faithful living that both draws from and enriches the wider church community. Theologian Flourence Caffrey Bourg, who has written extensively on the topic of the domestic church, argues that looking at our family life from this perspective can "stimulate imaginations to a deeper appreciation of the mystery of the Church and of how family life figures into God's plan of gracious presence in history."[19]

What is essential, in her view, is not looking at domestic church from the vantage point of organization or function, but from a place of vision: "[M]embers of domestic churches come to 'see' ordinary life as God's instrument for relating to them and as their medium for embodying love of God."[20] Caffrey Bourg understands this vision bespeaks an ideal, one we will fail not occasionally but regularly. But the vision is key to understanding that our marriages and family life do not take us away from moments of holiness—moments we may envision on mountaintops or retreat centers—

but rather, these relationships that shape our daily commitments are the very place in which we attempt holiness. Our homes are the places in which we encounter the daily "opportunity to be 'schooled' in the way of discipleship."[21] The lessons are as routine as "share with your brother" and as poignant as "I am truly sorry." We do not *go* to church; we *live* as church, and at times we celebrate that within our wider community.

Sacraments Call Us Outward: Counting the Shoes

To call our homes places we encounter the sacraments is to know God is not experienced only in moments and places set apart but in the very everydayness of life.[22] One man we met described it well, "This is real life. This is the nitty-gritty feeding the kids, going to work everyday; that's a sacrament too. And it's really important for the church to recognize that too and not just have us lowly peons looking up at the great sacraments up there. We need to realize what we are doing is really important for the world, really important for God and each other."

As sacrament, marriage and family life demonstrate God's grace in the world, most closely to those in the family, but as signs for the wider community as well. The strength of our marriage and family bonds calls us to extend ourselves in service to the communities of which we are a part. Reflecting on the work of theologian David Hollenbach, Hanlon Rubio notes: "If sharing food was Jesus' way of symbolizing his commitment to the earliest Christian community and, ultimately, to all people, Christians must also share food in and with their communities."[23]

One couple recalled an extended family member shaking his head as he noted, "I don't think there's a child in [this town] who has not eaten out of [your] refrigerator." Another woman explained the way she shared food with the community beyond her family: "My sons' friends would just come and take their shoes off and sleep here. I would always count how many shoes were at the door and then I'd know how much breakfast to make." While she did not express it this way, this act of counting the shoes is a sacrament, a sign of God's grace extending to those she was called to feed. We turn now to a deeper exploration of the ways our couples understand their marriages as the avenue through which they extend hospitality and serve the world around them.

"Jesus Showed Us How to Live"
Serving and Welcoming Neighbors

"The foundational message of Christianity is: you are not here for yourselves."[1] Presumably then, we are here for God and others. Christians are called to serve. We have touched on this theme already, both directly and indirectly. In chapter 1 on friendship, we discussed the place that self-sacrifice has in the married relationship. A good friend learns how to overcome selfishness and put the needs of the other first. In chapter 2 on *eros* and generativity, we examined the Catholic understanding of marriage as both unitive and life-giving, or generative. The communion that exists between married persons is not just for their own benefit, but for the good of the world; the love that married partners share is meant to overflow and bring life to others. In chapter 3, we highlighted the sacramental nature of marriage in the Catholic tradition. In their married relationship, and in their wider family lives, spouses encounter the living God. Further, married partners *become* sacrament to the world insofar as they live out the virtues and "bring more God into the world."

In this chapter, we will build on these ideas, furthering the notion that Christian marriage is other-centered and meant to serve God's purposes in the world. Specifically, we will discuss the role and importance of service and hospitality in Christian marriage, informed by Scripture and illustrated by the stories of the married couples in our study.

Matthew Murphy describes his wife, Margaret—who was working with developmentally disabled persons when they met—as a woman of "compassion."[2] He admires that, "The world is bigger than Margaret. Her world is bigger than herself." This compassionate openness to the world is apparent in how we heard Margaret define her marriage in chapter 3: "[O]ur marriage as sacrament . . . means very strongly that it cannot be, like the light under the bushel, an insular thing, a Matthew and me [thing], kind of like a me-and-Jesus kind of thinking, like it's all about me and Jesus." Margaret goes on to explain that this perspective is one that she and Matthew worked to share with their children:

> And we've always kind of tried to instill that with our kids even when they went from grade school to high school and out: that somehow that love, that compassion, it would be selfish for us just to keep it in our family and say, "Okay, we're all happy. Everybody's good." We always, we talk about this. That's our challenge. *Are we doing enough? Are we giving enough?* You know what I mean? It shouldn't be this big heavy guilt thing, but it should be a bit of a challenge and nudge that, *yeah, we're blessed, so what are we doing to extend that?* Our marriage should be a mirror of love to other people.

We are struck by the way that the love and compassion experienced *within* Margaret and Matthew's marriage and family moves them to show love and compassion *outside* of it. Margaret believes that the resources that she and Matthew have are not for their good alone, or even the good of their family; rather, their marriage is to mirror God's love ever-outward, by extending and sharing what they have with others. She identifies the temptation to simply be content with the satisfaction and happiness of their own family, or in Matthew's words, to "get too comfortable."

To fight this temptation, this couple practices a regular examination of conscience by asking themselves: What more can we do for others? What more can we give? How else might we extend our blessings? Note how Margaret explicitly holds the social component of her Christian faith in the forefront. For her, a personal relationship with Jesus—while foundational—must be reflected in her interactions with, and actions on behalf of, others. Her relationship with Jesus asks something more of her, and of her marriage and family.

Specifically, Margaret believes they must practice certain virtues that are rooted in the preaching and ministry of Jesus. She sees Jesus as the model for being and acting: "I always tell the kids that Jesus showed us how to live. It was his loving and being true to what he knew he had to do to bring justice, to bring peace, to bring love to the world. That's what got him in trouble. But we're called to do the same. The whole message of social justice: how do we bring that love and healing?"

Indeed: *Jesus showed us how to live.* He loved. He lived authentically, despite risk and rejection. He brought justice and peace. He healed. He washed feet. *We are called to do the same.*

A God of Mercy: Exceeding All Human Expectations

In Cardinal Kasper's recent work, he argues that mercy is "the funda-mental attribute of God."[3] The God who is revealed in the Bible, and most fully in Jesus Christ, is a God whose essence is mercy (*misericordia*). "The Latin word *misericordia*, according to its literal sense, means to have one's heart (*cor*) with the poor (*miseri*) or to have a heart for the poor."[4] To claim that God's essence is mercy, therefore, is to claim that God has a heart, or a special love, for the poor.

In the Hebrew Scriptures, the mercy of God is revealed through the prophets, who are sent by God to call for justice for the trampled-upon poor. Further, God shows a special love for the poor in the Exodus story: the enslaved people call out, and *God hears the cry of the poor* and takes action on their behalf, leading them out of slavery and into community. In fact, God treats the covenanted people mercifully again and again. We see the people turn from God repeatedly in spite of their promises to be faithful, but time and again, God forgives and mends relationship rather than punishing or severing relationship.

Cardinal Kasper asserts that God's mercy in the Hebrew Scriptures "exceeds all human expectations and bursts every human category." He writes: "To think that God, who is all-powerful and holy, concerns himself with the distressing and self-caused situation of human beings, that God sees the wretchedness of the poor and miserable people, that he hears their lament, that he bends down in condescension, that he descends to persons in their need and, despite every human infidelity, concerns himself with them again and again, and that he forgives them and gives them another chance, even though they had deserved just punishment—all of this exceeds normal human experience and expectation; all of this transcends human imagination and thought."[5] This God surprisingly—and in absolute free-dom—draws near to the people, especially those who are most in need, not because the people deserve it, but because they are profoundly loved by God and it is the nature of God to show mercy.

In the New Testament, we see the mercy of God further revealed through the words and actions of Jesus. Christians are familiar with many of the parables told by Jesus that reveal the merciful nature of God. Perhaps the finest example is the story of the Prodigal Son, the son who rejects his fa-ther, runs away, and squanders his inheritance, yet is treated with abundant mercy upon his return home.

Steve and Barbara Miller are recent empty-nesters, married twenty-six years, with two children, Greg and Molly. During our interview, Steve told a parable of his own about loving his children, that gave him—and, in turn, gave us—powerful insight into the merciful nature of God's love. As you will see, Steve relates his experience to the parable of the Prodigal Son:

> I understand the concept of preferential option for the poor in a different way because of our kids. What I mean by that is, you know how God loves us all, but you know *really* loves the person who is hurting or who is down and out and who does not have enough to eat, whatever, and our kids, you know, we love them both equally. They are both our kids and you can't say one is better than the other or anything like that. . . . I remember when Greg was a sophomore in college and he came home for Thanksgiving. We saw him for Thanksgiving dinner, and we saw him, I think, Friday morning, but we didn't see him again until he was leaving on Sunday. And we were *so incensed*. He didn't come home Friday night and he didn't come home Saturday night. He was out gallivanting. And we were so mad, and he left in a huff to go back to college. He didn't answer texts, and he didn't answer phone calls for a couple weeks, and we're looking at Christmas thinking this kid may not be coming home, and we may have lost this kid. We didn't know what to do. I called a school counselor just trying to figure out what to do with this kid. And he's ultimately an extremely good kid, but he was just having [a tough] time, right? So I talked to a friend of ours and she said, "Well why don't you just go see him? Just go see him unannounced, go up there." And it just struck me as, *are you kidding me?* And then I sat on that for a while and then I said, *Yeah, what would happen if I just went up there, drove the five plus hours, go over to his apartment and lay it on the line?* Molly was home in high school so she knew there was stress and a blowup going on here, so I had her get ahold of Greg and kind of feel out where he would be on a particular day. That day, knowing that he had class at a certain time, knowing he would be home at a certain time, I got in the car and drove. So, I (I am getting a little emotional here) went into his apartment and he just broke down, just totally lost it and I totally lost it as well, and it was just like the prodigal son kind of reunion of sorts, and I was so glad that I did that. That's what he needed at that time. I couldn't just treat him and Molly as if they were both equally in need at that time, because Molly was going through high school and she didn't need anything at that time, but he needed something special and so, making that sacrifice driving up there and driving back the same day—I just went up, we did that, we had dinner, I got in the car and drove back home. That's what was needed at that time. And

> I think of Molly right now, she's the person that needs the most right now and Greg is doing just fine, so I think kids teach us that lesson of preferential option for the poor: that they have different needs at different times and sometimes those needs are pretty great.

In loving his children concretely in the midst of changes and circumstances, Steve realized that showing his love *rightly* means treating their needs *preferentially*—the one who is hurting and most in need must be given priority of energy and care. Through his experience parenting, Steve gained insight into the theological concept of "a preferential option for the poor," that originated in Latin American liberation theology and is now prominent in Catholic social teaching. The concept highlights God's special concern for the poor and marginalized that is apparent in Scripture and is rooted in the idea that while God loves all human beings equally, in Steve's words, God "*really* loves the person who is hurting or who is down and out and who does not have enough to eat."

According to Catholic social teaching, the church itself, as well as every individual Christian, is obligated to make an option for the poor, to show the poor preference, to make sure that the marginalized have their needs met before the wants of the privileged are satisfied.[6] Steve and Barbara show mercy by meeting their children's needs—that vary in intensity—as best they can, "and sometimes those needs are pretty great." Loving their own children in this way causes them to better empathize with and respond to the concrete needs of people in the wider community, whom God profoundly loves in their need. In doing so, they "mirror" a merciful God who has a heart for the poor.

The lesson of meeting the other's needs with mercy is reinforced in the parable of the Good Samaritan. In the Gospels, Jesus tells his followers that the greatest commandment is the love commandment, on which "hangs all of the law and the prophets." That is, "You shall love the Lord your God with all your heart, and with all your soul, and with all your mind." And, "You shall love your neighbor as yourself" (Matt 22:36–40). When the disciples ask Jesus to specify—but, "Who is our neighbor?"—Jesus answers with the parable of the Good Samaritan. Christians likely know the story well: a Jewish man is attacked by robbers and left at the side of the road, beaten and bloody. A couple of apparently respectable and righteous men see the needy man but pass him by. They cannot be bothered or inconvenienced (perhaps, in their minds, for good reason). Surprisingly, the one who finally stops to help is a Samaritan, who typically would not have interacted with a

Jewish man nor seen him as a neighbor for whom he was responsible. Yet the Good Samaritan is merciful, bringing the man to safety and providing for his care. As it turns out, in this parable the neighbor is defined as "the one who shows mercy," the one who takes responsibility for the person in need.

Part of the power of this story is that it pushes the boundaries of those for whom we are responsible, shaking us out of the notion that it is only people in our inner circle, or people like ourselves, for whom we need care. The parable prompts us to ask, as Margaret and Matthew Murphy do, how we might "extend our blessings" or our circle of mercy.

A People of Mercy: Trying to See Jesus

Caring for Neighbors: I'm Serving Jesus

Steve Miller, who offered the parable above, takes the preferential option for the poor seriously in his own life. He identifies Dorothy Day as a "big spiritual hero" and has, over the past twenty years, "tried to involve [him]self in things that she probably would have been involved in." Indeed, Steve—with the support of his wife—has been very active in a variety of organizations and efforts that serve and advocate for persons who are homeless in his community. His direct service allows him to be "present in people's lives of all shapes and sizes" and to be "accepting of who they are [and] where they're at."

Steve explains: "The whole dimension of service, especially grounded in Matthew 25, has been a pretty big thing for our family." He and Barbara included their children from young ages in service, both indirect and direct. For example, their family chose a family in need through their parish each Christmastime and bought gifts for the family, and on occasion Steve and Barbara took their children to work with them at a community shelter, so that the "whole dimension of Jesus saying we came to serve not to be served . . . [was and] is the underpinning of their family life."

Steve mentions Matthew 25 as grounding their family's understanding of service. Matthew 25 includes the parable of the Last Judgment, in which Jesus specifies what is required in order to "gain eternal life." According to this parable, those who feed the hungry, give drink to the thirsty, welcome the stranger, clothe the naked, care for the sick, and visit the imprisoned will "inherit the kingdom." Further, when one ministers to any person who is hungry, thirsty, estranged, naked, ill, or imprisoned, one ministers to Christ: "whatsoever you did for the least of my people, you did for me." Because the actions mentioned in the parable focus on bodily needs, the Christian tradition named them (along with the requirement to bury the dead) "the corporal works of mercy."[7] Cardinal Kasper notes that this story teaches us that "one can sin not only by violating God's commandments, but also by failing to do what is good," by refusing to be attentive and sensitive to the concrete needs we encounter.[8]

Matthew 25 informs the service of Sophia Vandenbusch, who works with the elderly, specifically older persons with special needs. While not naming the parable of the Last Judgment explicitly, Sophia referenced it when telling us that, "in working with a population of people who are sick, who are needy, and who are sometimes challenging . . . I have that voice in my head, pretty consistently, of trying to see Jesus. I will think it in my head as I am talking to them: I am serving Jesus."

She described to us a particular incident at a Catholic nursing home that vividly connects to the parable: "There was an elderly woman who hollered out all the time, and so she was ignored all the time. This was actually a Catholic building. So she was hollering out, and I can't remember if she was asking for water or just hollering out, but whatever it was, I went over to her, and it turned out she needed something to drink because the host was stuck to her tongue, and I remember just feeling overwhelmed that that was Jesus talking to me."

It may seem strange to hear Sophia speak of being "overwhelmed" by Jesus "talking to [her]" through this simple interaction, but she is perceptively identifying the sacramental depth of the experience. Interpreted through the eyes of faith, Sophia recognizes the holiness of the ordinary—in this case a woman calling out in thirst and being offered something to drink. Sophia—shaped by the stories of the faith and her practice of looking for Jesus in the people that she serves—is able to see the presence of Jesus Christ in the elderly woman, as well as in the Eucharist that rests on her tongue. Further, Sophia seizes the opportunity to become Christ-like when she mercifully quenches the woman's thirst and affirms her dignity. Ironically, the elderly woman who finds it difficult to communicate to the point that she is usually ignored is the one who communicates the presence of Jesus with such clarity.

Sophia told us, "I am very fortunate" that interacting with people in need "is part of what I do because the opportunity [to serve] is there all the time."

While this is true in Sophia's case, in our conversations with couples we found that opportunities to serve neighbors abound, even when one is not in an occupation that caters to the marginalized—whether it be neighbors next door, in one's parish or local community, or across the world in an underdeveloped or war-torn country. Couples in our study serve their neighbors in myriad ways; for example, ministering in hospitals and nursing homes, working at homeless shelters, raising money for cancer research and other charities, planning fundraisers for ill friends, participating in service trips here or abroad, bringing the Eucharist to the homebound, volunteering in parishes and schools, organizing and distributing food at pantries, and more. The people we interviewed clearly understand such activities to be forms of "service." Additionally, while folks are less likely to call it "service," we heard story upon story about reaching out to neighbors who are sick or elderly, whether it be shoveling snow, "checking in" to ensure safety and well-being, or delivering groceries.

One couple told us about caring for two elderly women who lived in town; the couple took the two women shopping regularly for "at least ten years." To be sure, that kind of long-term attention to one's neighbors takes discipline. John and Nancy Brady do the weekly grocery shopping for a family friend, Rita, who is 102 and does not have any family in town. John explains that while there is a routine aspect to shopping and dropping off groceries, there is more to it than simple routine. "I mean, I never just go, 'Oh, hi. I'm here. Do you have your list? Okay, thanks.' We visit. So whenever I go to pick up the list, which I usually do because it is on my way to work and back, I tell Nancy that I am stopping at Rita's—we know it's going to be a while. I sit down, chit chat. I think it's more, it's a lot more than we just do the grocery shopping, for her, and for me, too. . . . It is a social thing. We are doing her a service, so to speak, but more than just the physical groceries."

John recognizes that they are caring for Rita as a person, feeding her body *and* her spirit. And the nourishment of spirit is reciprocal. John and Nancy appreciate how invested Rita is in their family; she has no grandchildren of her own but takes "great joy" in the Brady children. She is interested in all of the children's activities and is concerned about the well-being of their entire family. One day when Nancy could not bring the groceries but forgot to call Rita, she got a concerned phone call, "I just love you guys so much and I just wanted to make sure nothing was wrong!"

It was a reminder to Nancy and John of the importance of their relationship with Rita, even though it can be inconvenient to maintain the shopping routine when they have dual-careers and a family of their own. Nancy is honest about the difficulty of caring for Rita's needs on a regular basis. "For me, sometimes, quite frankly, it's kind of a pain to do it. Because it's been years now and I have to worry about her grocery shopping on top of ours. And sometimes, I'm like, *Really? Can't we just go to the grocery store and get what I need because I'm in a hurry and have had a very busy week*, or whatever. And it keeps me grounded in [the call that] we're supposed to be taking care of other people. This is what our lives are about. God puts us here to take care of others and not just be in our own little bubble. So it helps, for me individually, to reinforce that idea of reaching out to other people and to care for other people."

Sophia Vandenbusch admires how her husband, Mike, "goes out of his way to help the neighbors. He goes above and beyond. He's the first guy out there shoveling snow, or moving mulch, or our neighbor down the street, she's a grandma, ninety-six, she just passed away, but she'd love to do the sewing. She would tease me that I couldn't even sew on a button (which is probably true!), but we kept up the façade, because it was really important to Mike, which I thought was wonderful. He just gave her stuff to sew all the time because it made her happy." Mike added, "It was stuff that I would have thrown away, but Gram wants to sew." Mike and Sophia laughed as they described all of the patches on Mike's clothes—big patches on jeans and t-shirts. Although Gram has died, Mike still wears the mended clothes proudly. They are a gift from their beloved neighbor, who, by sewing, felt useful and showed her care. Mike's way of caring for her was insightful: to allow *her* to care for *him*.

These examples of care for neighbor make it clear that there are different kinds of poverty, and that being merciful need not mean participating in some sort of organized service project. When one makes an option for the poor, one might practice the corporal works of mercy, but one might also practice the spiritual works of mercy, caring for the spirit of the person in need. Kasper describes a "lack of relationships" as a form of poverty. "As a social creature, the human person can experience various forms of poverty: loneliness and isolation, the loss of a partner, the loss of family members or friends, communication difficulties, exclusion from social intercourse—whether self-caused or forced upon a person—discrimination and marginalization, including the extreme cases of isolation or exile."[9] If we return to Margaret's question: how do we bring love and healing? The answer depends on which neighbor is being served and whether the person's poverty is bodily or spiritual.

Extending Hospitality: You Just Have to Share It

One valuable way that the couples in our study have met both the bodily and spiritual needs of their neighbors is by extending hospitality. By hospitality, we are not simply referring to having friends and family over for a dinner party. While entertaining friends and loved ones *is* a form of hospitality and is no doubt enjoyable, even enriching, we are discussing here a form of hospitality that is deeper, more substantive, and certainly more challenging. We are referring to the virtue of Christian hospitality. Christine Pohl, professor of Christian ethics, explains that the distinctive quality of Christian hospitality is "that it offers a generous welcome to the 'least' without concern for advantage or benefit to the host. Such hospitality reflects God's greater hospitality that welcomes the undeserving, provides the lonely with a home, and sets a banquet table for the hungry."[10]

Pohl conducted an extensive study in which she interviewed contemporary practitioners of Christian hospitality (for example, people who live and work in Catholic Worker houses of hospitality or L'Arche communities in which able-bodied persons live in community with persons with disabilities). She found that the Scripture passage that was most often quoted by these practitioners is: "I was a stranger and you welcomed me," from the Parable of the Last Judgment. Christian hospitality is most fundamentally about welcoming the stranger. But who is the stranger that needs to be welcomed? Pohl helpfully explains that the stranger is not just a person that you do not yet know who may be on the other end of the room at some social gathering. Rather, "strangers, in the strict sense, are those who are disconnected from basic relationships that give persons a secure place in the world. The most vulnerable strangers are detached from family, community, church, work and polity. This condition is most clearly seen in the state of homeless people and refugees. Others experience detachment and exclusion to lesser degrees."[11] The stranger, then, is the one who is disenfranchised, defenseless, excluded, disconnected—often without a safety net. Thus, Christian hospitality is reaching out to strangers, making them feel welcome, worthy, included, and secure.

We were deeply moved by the many stories of hospitality that we heard from couples, that include working with homeless persons in the community; ministering to people with special needs; housing needy friends, loved ones, or strangers; including vulnerable family members who may otherwise be left out; adopting children who are especially vulnerable; and, "adopting" or creating a place of welcome for members of the community who are "on the margins."

For example, one woman expressed profound gratitude for her husband, Craig, who extended hospitality to her sister, Lizzie, while they were dating. "My sister was diabetic and lost her eyesight when she was twenty-three. And when she did, she lost all of her friends. In those days, people didn't know how to handle it, so they just didn't come over. And so Craig and I were dating, and every time we went out, we took Lizzie. So here I am dating somebody that takes me *and* my sister out; every single weekend we went out together. . . . Craig never once said, 'Well, it would be really nice to go somewhere without your sister.' He never once did that."

Another woman, Patricia, praises the goodness of her husband, Dan, who agreed to take in her brother, who is disabled, to permanently live with their family.[12]

> He's my older brother. And when he asked to come live with us, I gave him a year before I said, "okay." But in that time I said, "Let's see if a year down the road you still want to come live with us." He would come to visit and he didn't want to go back home. And we were in the middle of having our third child when he came to live with us. So we went from three kids to essentially four. . . . I don't know how many people would take in a brother-in-law for the rest of their lives . . . our kids are going to grow up and go away, but my brother is not. And Dan is really good to him. It's challenging a lot of the time, and being his sister is challenging. But on Dan's part, I think it takes a lot for someone to do that . . . and, like I said, Dan is really good to him.

"He's been good for the kids, too," replied Dan. "I think it's good for the whole family." "Yeah," responded Patricia. "But it's challenging nonetheless. It's not an easy thing."

The adoption story of Jerry and Lisa Simms is another excellent example of Christian hospitality. Lisa spent time as a young person working with children with special needs and dreamed of someday adopting a child from foster care, knowing that "it comes with a lot of baggage." From the time they were engaged, she expressed that wish to Jerry. Twelve years into their marriage, with their "hands full" raising two sons, they decided to pursue the adoption of an older child out of the foster care system. It was important to Lisa and Jerry that it be a family decision and that their sons be fully supportive of the idea. They broached the subject with their boys (who were twelve and nine years old at the time) on their way to a birthday party out of town, so "they were all trapped together in the car." They tried to be as honest as possible about what this kind of adoption might mean for their family. Jerry and Lisa explained to their sons:

> Not every child has a family. And that there are children out there who are neglected and abused. And at that time, at their age, they may not have fully comprehended that there are some kids that

need a mom and a dad or a big brother. [We] just [tried] to make them aware that there are these situations out there, and it may not be easy, and if you had a child like that come into your home they might break all your toys. They might destroy something that you care about. And that there's potential for all these other issues, and we don't know what all those issues might be, but that we will work together on them.

The boys were also told outright that adopting a child with special needs would demand financial sacrifices from the family. Lisa said to the boys, "Other families are going to go to Disneyworld; we're not going to do that. Is that okay? You need to think about that. We'll still go camping. We'll do things, fun things, but we're not going to have big trips and fancy stuff." The boys also were told that they might have to share a room together. Lisa explained, "They were okay with that."

In fact, the boys were "on board" from the very beginning "and never lost their excitement." They agreed from the start to make necessary sacrifices in order to bring a new sibling into their family. Jerry mentioned that, during their initial conversation with the boys, one of them "thought he could pick a little sister and name her, so it took a little bit to talk him out of that. Because it was 'well, this child will already have a name, you know, you don't get to change it.'"

This moment is significant. Jerry and Lisa clarified that the family would be making room for a *particular person*, who already had a name and a (difficult) history. A lovely sign of the boys' willingness to "make room" was that on the very day they first discussed adopting with their parents in the van—the day they made a family decision to move forward—"[the boys] came home and packed up all their special things in a box . . . and then they moved into the same room together." Because they were told they might have to share a room when a new sibling came, "they did it that day. They packed up their stuff and moved into the same room. And then we waited two more years." Lisa recollected that one of their sons found a wall hanging "with that reading from Samuel, 'For this child I have prayed.' And he put it in [the empty room], too." For two and a half years "that other room was ready and waiting" for the arrival of their brother.

Jerry and Lisa Simms are proud of their older sons, who "were on board 100 percent from day one," and encouraged their parents to maintain hope during the long, and often discouraging, adoption process. Since the adoption, the boys "have been so supportive. They will work with him, play with him. And they're so patient. They've grown up a lot as well."

Each member of this family has become more virtuous as a result of practicing hospitality—that is, through the process of welcoming the once-stranger who is now *son* and *brother*, who is now rooted in family and home. For Jerry and Lisa, as for Patricia and Dan, extending hospitality has been—and continues to be—challenging, yes, but also "good for the whole family."

Many other couples and families have opened their doors regularly to family, friends, even strangers in need. For example, Frank and Kelly Brown recently hosted their daughter's classmate for several weeks because his mom, who is an Iraqi refugee, had the opportunity to make a return visit to Iraq. The daughter's friend is only one of the many people who have stayed with the Browns in a time of need; in fact, they see hospitality as an essential value and are intentional about expanding the boundaries of their home in a way that "includes others, considers others, and cares for others."

Likewise, Jack and Gretchen Baker see hospitality as a way to share the gifts they have been given by God. Over twenty years ago, with three boys of their own, they took in a niece when she was nineteen, pregnant, unmarried, and without any place to go. Gretchen told her niece, "'Come and live with me; we'll figure it out.' I had no idea it was going to be for the rest of my life, but God doesn't tell you, so" [laughter]. She and Jack talked about their hospitality nonchalantly, as "just what families do."

Jack and Gretchen both came from large families themselves—with nine siblings each—and, Jack noted, "As a large family you put up; it's not about you or anything else—it's about family." In their families they learned to care for one another, share what they have, and deal with the unexpected. Jack added, "I think our faith has taught us that what we have is borrowed, it's loaned to us. We've done things for it and everything else, but it's really been given to us as a gift to share, so really the only thing you have to do in life then is figure out how to share it. Some people don't want to share it, so they build a barn and put it all in it instead of sharing it. But when you finally realize that you just have to share it, it makes it a lot easier."

Clare and Rick Bender took in Clare's sister, June, after Clare's mother died. June was living with her father, which "was hard on her. He was never home." When their father remarried, June did not get along with her stepmother and asked to live with Clare and Rick, who already were raising six children in "not a real big house." June was in high school and "went through a lot of tough times." Admittedly, Clare and Rick worried about her influence on their own children, but they nevertheless brought June into their home and raised her until she graduated from high school. Rick told us, "It was hard to discipline her. But I think the reason it worked is because we always did it together. If we ran into something, we discussed it and we did it together. It worked."

In chapter 3, we mentioned Dan and Roseann Carr who have an "open-door policy" with kids and have been accused of feeding every child in their town at some point. For about six months, when Roseann's brother's family was building a new house, her brother moved his family into Dan and Roseann's house. The brother and his wife brought four kids, a dog, a guinea pig, and two fish! If you add that to Dan and Roseann's own brood, that is a very full house. It is clear that hospitality is an essential virtue for the Carrs. When introducing themselves, Dan said, "We have three children and a part-time child that we took in years ago. We have three biological grandchildren and nine that we take care of, let's put it that way."

Dan and Roseann seem to be experts at providing hospitality, though they did not use that word to describe their experience. The "part-time child" that they raised came to them unexpectedly. Roseann explained, "When our middle son was fourteen or fifteen, he came home with a friend one night and said, 'Can Timmy stay here with us tonight? He's having some issues at home. His Dad told him he needed to get out. He'll be going back tomorrow.' Timmy is now twenty-eight-years-old and he never went back home. He's been a part of our life, and we had a lot of issues with him, *a lot* of issues." Timmy's biological parents struggled with substance abuse; his dad is an alcoholic, and his mom a drug addict. Roseann told us, "When Timmy first came and we gave him an eleven o'clock curfew, he asked, 'What's a curfew?' Nobody cared that he was coming home. He had tears in his eyes because nobody cared when he came home." Dan and Roseann *did* care when Timmy came home; they became Timmy's hands-on parents and held him responsible in the same way that they did their biological sons.

Still, as Roseann mentioned, the family had "a lot of issues" with Timmy over the years; he has had his own substance abuse problems and has been in and out of jail. While there were moments when Roseann and Dan wanted to "throw in the towel," instead they "stuck by him"—visiting Timmy in jail, providing a home base when he was not incarcerated, hoping and praying for a better future for him, and continuing to love him in the midst of struggles. Timmy has been sober for a number of years and is married with three children of his own, but in Dan's words, he will always need some "moral corralling." Dan and Roseann plan to be there to provide that for him.

Bob and Jeanne Mitchell have also taken responsibility for a young person who is in need of moral guidance and care. In this case, the young man came out of the foster care system and has been in and out of prison.

Bob, in particular, has served as a mentor for him, but both Bob and Jeanne have worked with him "prettily steadily over the last ten years." Because of the demands of this relationship and the difficulty of maintaining it, Jeanne said, "It sometimes feels like we do that because of what we think faithfulness looks like." Bob added, "Yeah, without a doubt. We're motivated by a calling, to family in a sense, I mean he doesn't have any family. In a sense he doesn't have anybody. And if it weren't for our faith and the way we understand that to be, we would not, I would not, be involved with him. Because he wouldn't be my first choice. But having said that, I said to somebody once: I think my salvation, or my redemption, is tied to him. I don't know what I mean by that exactly, but it made sense to me when I said it."

Bob's conviction that his redemption is somehow tied to the hospitality that he shows to this man seems to make sense in light of the Parable of the Last Judgment. Bob is living out the Gospel demand to welcome the stranger, which is how one "inherits the kingdom"—the young man he mentors is a stranger in the strict sense of the word, disenfranchised and devoid of community.[13] Despite the challenges of this relationship, that are many, Bob and Jeanne continue to practice hospitality and show fidelity because they believe God calls them to do so.

The Carters also feel called by God to be hospitable. Mark Carter—who married his wife, Joanne, thirty-three years ago—brought tears to her eyes when he said, "Joanne is the most tremendous human being. She has a heart as big as this room and she loves more than anybody else I've ever known."

Joanne beautifully expresses that love through hospitality. When Mark and Joanne's three boys were young, the Carter house was a "McGruff house," that "was a safe house for [their] neighborhood." When new families would come into their neighborhood, the Carters would go greet them with cookies, and let the parents know that their children would be welcome and safe at the Carter's home. In a different way, the Carter house is a "safe house" today, especially for people within the LGBTQ community. Mark and Joanne's oldest son, Charlie, came out as gay when he was in high school. Mark and Joanne are very active Catholics who work in Catholic parishes, and once word got out that Charlie was gay, other parents with LGBTQ children would approach the Carters. Joanne explained:

> People at church would come to me and say, [whispering] "We have something in common." And I'm thinking, *The age of our mothers? The street we live on? What could it be?* You know, it was like pulling teeth to get them to say it. I would ask, "Do you have a gay

or lesbian child?" "Yes!" [They would whisper]. The first one, a seventy-nine or eighty-year-old married woman said, "I love the Eucharist. I love my child. I love my grown child. She is forty-three and a grown child. She's—what am I going to do?" She says, "I don't know what to do. The church says this, and I know this." I thought to myself, *Oh my word*. She just had an effect on me. Then another person said something, then another, then another, and it just kept happening, so here we are.

Joanne now leads a support group for Catholic parents of LGBTQ children that meets monthly to talk and share experiences. "And boy," said Joanne, "I have to say that our circle of friends has just opened wide. Talk about a blessing." In addition to the hospitality extended through the parental support group, Mark told us that he and Joanne "make sure our home is a place where people can come. There are still people—friends of ours and community people—who just don't feel like they are welcome in places. At least people feel welcome in our home. We try to make sure of that . . . [though] it's not always clean. Just the fact that—'Yes, when you want to come over, come. Sit down and we'll talk.'"

For the Carters, the condition of their house is much less important than providing an open invitation to their home, in which all guests are embraced in their authenticity, as sons and daughters of God, especially those who are made to feel unwelcome elsewhere.[14]

Models of Mercy: The Parish Beyond Trivia Night

"I think the witness of our pastor shows us that this is a place where Christian values are seriously lived," said Kathleen Cotter during her focus group. The rest of the participants nodded enthusiastically. "The pastoral leadership matters. We are a wonderful parish community, but we need, we all need to see that . . . we don't do it all by ourselves." The group discussed for some time the way that their pastor is an inspirational model of mercy for them:

Thomas O'Brien: Father Jim is not perfect. . . .

Kathleen Cotter: No, he'll tell you that!

Thomas: [B]ut, he's a saint. [Again, nods around the table. "Yes!" "That's true!"]. He is an extraordinary guy who has embodied the gospel in such a way that he doesn't have to . . . he sometimes reads a talk, but he doesn't need to, it just boils out of him. ["Yes!" "Yes!" from others.] And that kind of person, you don't run into very often.

Mary O'Brien: You're right, he's not just talking about it. He is up at the immigration center. He is with the police department, the fire department.

Thomas: And he likes to talk about it: "Yesterday when I was with this person who was dying. And the day before when I witnessed. . . ." . . . it's very real ["It's real." "It's very real," called out the others.]

Kathleen, looking at her husband: I remember when you were doing overnight work at the hospital. . .

Jeremy Cotter: Yeah. We didn't have a priest on staff so we had priests around the area who rotated being on call. So it was the middle of the night and I got answering machine, answering machine, answering machine, and then Fr. Jim picked up. The middle of the night and he answered his phone. I explained the situation and he said, "I'll be there." ["That's him!" someone called out in affirmation. "That's leadership."]

These parishioners lovingly describe their pastor as "a saint." Though imperfect, he is a man who embodies gospel values and who shows mercy to those in need, no matter the inconvenience. Fr. Jim's witness as "a real human being who shares his own struggles and his own self and can walk the walk" of challenging gospel values is an inspiration. He models mercy and, through actions more than words, calls his parishioners to be merciful in turn.

We heard from folks in other parishes about "good leadership" that inspires involvement and commitment to gospel values. In one focus group we heard about a leadership team, consisting of a priest and two religious sisters, that calls "everyone to be involved and be active and help out" and that serves as a model of mercy.

A focus group participant told the story of a family friend, Billy, who "probably hadn't been to church since he was twelve. And he got cancer. When he was in the hospital—this is when he was dying—they put down that he was Catholic. He told his girlfriend to put down that he was Catholic. And Father George showed up there and gave him the sacrament of healing, showed up every day until he died. And he and the two sisters did Billy's service. And the thing is—that's the kind of people they are. It didn't matter that Billy didn't come back until just before he died . . . that's how the people in this parish are."

Visit the sick. Bury the dead. This pastoral team practices the works of mercy, and it meant something to Billy, but is also meaningful to other members of the parish. It is not surprising, then, to hear: "We have a lot of parishioners who are involved in social justice issues and get others involved because of the [pastoral team's] leadership."

It is clear from our study that some parishes successfully foster service and hospitality by providing good leadership, fostering Christian virtues and values in liturgy and programming, offering prayer groups and other small faith groups that build community and promote service to the poor, and providing concrete opportunities for parishioners to practice hospitality and serve.

Yet theologian Julie Hanlon Rubio cautions that parishes in middle-class America may not be doing enough to encourage parishioners to take responsibility for the poor. She notes that certain activities that seem typical in parishes today, such as sports events, social events for young people, and fundraisers (e.g., auctions, carnivals and trivia nights) "require large investments of parishioners' time and, increasingly, their money," while doing little to challenge families "to live more simply out of solidarity with the oppressed."[15] Rubio acknowledges that there *are* activities in some parishes that "push adult Catholics" to actively take responsibility for the poor and marginalized—JustFaith is one example, along with "bible study groups, prayer groups, and small faith communities."[16] The majority of the couples that we spoke to were, in fact, involved in parish groups such as these. But Rubio indicates that the numbers of adult Catholics participating in such groups is actually quite small, around 5 percent.[17]

We acknowledge that (because of our methodology) the couples that completed our written surveys and those who participated in our interviews may be within the 5 percent referenced by Rubio. Nevertheless, we were impressed both by the amount of service that these couples did, organized and otherwise, and by the opportunities provided within their parishes for (indirect and direct) service work as well as spiritual support for that work, such as Bible studies and prayer groups.

We affirm Rubio's belief that parishes ought to actively teach (by word and example) mercy as a core gospel value and provide opportunities to live out a preferential option for the poor. Parishes that function in a way that effectively makes them middle- or upper-class social enclaves are antithetical to the gospel, and asking parishioners to give the bulk of their volunteer time and resources to support those enclaves—at the expense of the needy—is harmful. In contrast, we offer the stories of the couples in our study as models of service and hospitality, as models of what is "going right" in our parishes, with the hope that they will inspire others to practice mercy.

A Quick Note About Limits and Boundaries

Before closing this chapter, we would like to discuss briefly some practical considerations about service and hospitality in married and family life. Perhaps it seems obvious, but we think it important to note that *how* one serves depends on one's various responsibilities and station in life. For instance, we heard from many retired people that, since retirement, they have newly committed to more extensive service and "want to give back" now that they have the time to do so.

Sheila Pickard, who has been married to Brian for fifty years, explained how their commitment to service beyond their own family has changed over the years:

> We had four children in less than five years. Brian was the one who did [the volunteering]—he was head of the PTA and all of this stuff and a baseball coach. I don't think you can have both parents involved in those things. Somebody's got to be at home doing the ordinary stuff; putting the meal on the table, whatever. It's not very glamorous. We didn't find that we could both be involved in those things at the same time when our kids were young. Once you're older, I'm retired now, retired people are the people who are volunteering. We work the food pantry and that community shelter service and that sort of thing. But you can do that once you don't have the obligations that you have to your children and to each other.

Sheila's experience was echoed by other parents whose time to serve outside the home was limited when their children were small. Some couples found ways to "tag team" so that each could do some service in the community while raising children. Others did what Sheila and Brian did—essentially relying on one to care for home and children so that the other could "represent" the couple by doing volunteer work in schools, the parish, or the wider community.

One mother, whose husband worked as a truck driver and therefore was on the road often, admitted that she was not able to do service work in the community because she was working full-time as a teacher and caring for her young children while her husband was away. But she rightly saw her teaching as a form of service, and with the responsibilities she carried at home, this was surely enough.

Christian couples and families should not close in on themselves and refuse to see their neighbors' needs—in Margaret Murphy's words, families should not declare a self-satisfied "Okay, we're all happy. Everybody's good." Instead, they should extend mercy beyond their family boundary in imitation of our merciful God. At the same time, they rightly should be aware of the limits of their time and resources. Couples, together, ought to carefully discern what is required of them, and also what is possible for them in light of their varied commitments and circumstances. There are many needs in our families and in our communities, and "sometimes those needs are great," so couples must prudentially determine how to show mercy appropriately.

Since Jeremy Cotter's words began this chapter, it seems fitting to end the chapter with some sage advice from his wife, Kathleen: "One thing about the service and the going out: it is totally critical that you take care of your relationship, that you guard your relationship, that you put time in it to strengthen it and not try to be everything to everybody else . . . we really saw that in intentional community . . . if you don't have anything to give, you don't have anything to give. And you can only have something to give when you've taken care of the nuclear family and yourself."

5

Inescapable Pain

Encountering Suffering in Family Life

One of our survey respondents, a man married twenty-seven years, described the maturity and faithfulness required of long-lasting marriages. He summed up his perspective like this, "Marriage is not for punks!" We agree! Marriages thrive in the context of effort and courage; no "punks" allowed. Indeed, the couples we surveyed saw a role for courage in successful marriages: 43 percent indicated courage was extremely important to the success of their marriage, with an additional 38 percent finding it somewhat important. This cardinal virtue[1] is manifest in daily living; it takes courage to care for children, to challenge your spouse when you think he or she is wrong, to face daily setbacks, and to navigate complex schedules and commitments.

Matthew Murphy helped us understand the way couples experience courage in their marriages: "I guess if you did a free association, courage would conjure up battlefields. It's often used in a context of bravery. But I really do believe courage is about surrender. Not battle, but surrender."

Surrender. Indeed, this is the courage a loving marriage commitment requires—opening oneself first to the vulnerability of deep relationship with another and then openness to the inevitable suffering a life together will include. In this chapter we explore this connection between love and vulnerability, the pursuit of meaning in experiences of suffering, suffering viewed from the perspective of paschal mystery, and the ways that support—from one's spouse and the wider community—make it possible to emerge from suffering intact.

Where Love and Vulnerability Collide: Letting Your Spouse In

In *The Four Loves*, C. S. Lewis lays out the connection between love and vulnerability:

There is no safe investment. To love at all is to be vulnerable. Love anything, and your heart will certainly be wrung and possibly be broken. If you want to be sure of keeping it intact, you must give your heart to no one, not even an animal. Wrap it carefully round with hobbies and little luxuries; avoid all entanglements; lock it up safe in the casket or coffin of your selfishness. But in the casket—safe, dark, motionless, airless—it will change. It will not be broken; it will become unbreakable, impenetrable, irredeemable. The alternative to tragedy, or at least the risk of tragedy, is damnation. The only place outside Heaven where you can be perfectly safe from all dangers and perturbations of love is Hell.[2]

Indeed, entering into a loving relationship is only possible when we put ourselves at risk emotionally, when we disclose what we feel, or fear, or hope. Social psychologist Brené Brown calls vulnerability "the core, the heart, the center, of meaningful human experiences."[3]

Jeanne Carter spoke with us about an experience of vulnerability she shared with her husband Mark on a retreat for married couples: "[On this retreat] you have to share, even deeper than sharing sex with your spouse . . . share your deepest prayers and your deepest fears." She acknowledges couples often do not share at the level they were asked to on the retreat, but years later she and Mark are still impacted; they both nod as she concludes "that whole weekend was about opening up and letting your spouse in."

Matthew Murphy understands opening up to his wife Margaret is challenging at times. "[I]f there is something difficult you want to share with your spouse or if you're struggling through something that you feel you're trying to forgive yourself for—[it takes effort] . . . to really share your authentic self, the good, the bad, and the otherwise."

Sharing with your spouse your fears or prayers, or exposing that for which you feel you cannot forgive yourself evokes Brown's definition of vulnerability as "uncertainty, risk, and emotional exposure."[4] She goes on to describe the risk of loving vulnerably: "Waking up every day and loving someone who may or may not love us back, whose safety we can't ensure, who may stay in our lives or may leave without a moment's notice, who may be loyal to the day they die or betray us tomorrow—that's vulnerability. Love is uncertain. It's incredibly risky. And loving someone leaves us emotionally exposed."[5]

Phil and Jane Rullo married over fifty years ago, and today they delight in their grown children and grandchildren who live not far from their neighborhood. When we asked this devoted couple to share what sustains a long and loving marriage, Phil turned to the language of vulnerability: "One thing I think you have to do in marriage and love obviously is to learn to accept vulnerability and to find out some way of living with that comfortably." We invited him to share more about vulnerability, and he had much wisdom to offer:

> I don't think you can love without accepting vulnerability—if you are not going to accept vulnerability then you are never going to fall in love because you have to open yourself and become vulnerable to receive love. It is as simple as that. It is difficult: why do we always want the other person to say, "I love you" first. Why? Because we don't want to become vulnerable! "Well, you told me you love me and so. . ." Pass blame on the other person instead of on yourself. For me, it's a great step that's like Kierkegaard's leap of faith. Either you become vulnerable or you don't. If you don't become vulnerable, you're not a good lover.

We love not in order to avoid suffering but despite the awareness that being vulnerable to another may bring suffering. Lewis reminds us that our call as Christians is not that of careful self-protection: "Christ did not teach and suffer that we might become . . . more careful of our own happiness. . . . We shall draw nearer to God, not by trying to avoid the sufferings inherent in all loves, but by accepting them and offering them to Him; throwing away all defensive armour."[6] The couples we met entered into the risk of vulnerability with one another; in return life offered them struggles and pains to navigate together.

Suffering and Meaning: We Did What We Had to Do

We met couples who endured hardships of various types and severity. One must always tread carefully if attempting to measure suffering, but when we speak of severity here, we mean it not in terms of a measurement we have imposed but of the couples' own evaluations. Many had stories of financial distress to tell, but they tended to share these as though they were not significant concerns.[7] As one husband told us, in the early days of their marriage there were enough bills in his wallet, but "the numbers on the bills were too small!"

A woman more than fifty years into marriage looked back at the humble beginnings she and her husband shared: "So we bought this car—his parents loaned us the money. I was pregnant with our first child. We had no money. Everything we owned was in this car and we're going across some desert, maybe it was in Texas. I don't know where it was, and I said: 'Gee, what if we have a flat tire?' He said, 'It doesn't matter, we don't have a jack.' [Both laugh heartily.] And I said, 'Okay!' I mean that's just the way our life started out."

In one focus group the smallest family had only five children; the largest, nine! This group had plenty to say about finances. One woman offered, "If you wait to have children to afford them, you will never have them. You never have enough money. There is always something. You can't make sure you'll have enough; you'll never have enough." The woman next to her nodded vigorously in agreement, "No, you'll never have enough. That's just the reality." And her husband concurred, "Right."

For another couple, finances got tight when the husband lost his job as his wife entered her third trimester of pregnancy. Yet another couple spoke of several experiences of unemployment, each one invoking what they called a "no-spending streak." These were difficult each time, but especially the year the husband was laid off in November, and the couple faced Christmas with young children and no money to spend. The woman looked into the distance as she conjured up the memory: "So that was a little scary, too, but it drew us together. Tragedies always make us stronger."

Whether or not tragedies, in fact, *always* make us stronger, we see in this woman's comments the search for meaning in the experience of difficulty. Indeed, while such stories of financial troubles conjured up difficult times, more often than not, couples told these tales of woe with some happy conclusion, some version of humor or hope or perseverance: they made it through.

In *The Saints' Guide to Happiness: Everyday Wisdom from the Lives and Lore of the Saints*, Robert Ellsberg writes of the place of meaning in moments of suffering: "The saints do not teach us how to avoid suffering; they teach us how to suffer. They do not provide the 'meaning' of suffering. But they lived by the assurance that there is a meaning or truth at the heart of life that suffering is powerless to destroy."[8]

Deeply convinced of the goodness of God even despite hardship in life, such saints "found that there is no place that is literally 'godforsaken,' but that in every situation, even the most grim and painful, there is a door that leads to love, to faithfulness of life . . . to happiness."[9] It is with this type of vision that couples create a narrative in which suffering has left them stronger, has brought them closer together.

Looking back some fifty years, Ted Peterson explained, "When our first child was born, on that day I got laid off." His wife Paula chimed in, "It didn't bother us a bit. That was too bad, but he would find a job. The Lord was with us; our baby was healthy. We were young. We didn't let it faze us and God was on our side."

Some might see the loss of a job on the day a child is born as a *godforsaken* moment. But like the saints Ellsberg describes, the Petersons understood God was with them; their faith made them confident they would be alright in the end.

While the couples we met experienced suffering in varied ways, the stories that most often brought tears were those of illness and death, facing the end of life of a beloved parent or experiencing the loss of a child. With Sandy and Jim Paulson, the sadness and tension still seemed raw as they narrated the dying process of Jim's father, who lived on the other side of the state and for years battled the Parkinson's that would claim him. The anguish was palpable for this couple as they recalled both Jim's sadness in watching his father's diminishment and the difficulty Sandy faced as a working mother with young children whose husband needed to leave town every weekend. She told us, "We were busy during the week and he felt like he should go there because [his siblings] were there caring for his dad and it was kind of a rough time."

Sandy's description of this as "kind of a rough time" seems an understatement, as the Paulsons dealt with this situation over the course of more than two years. In the end, they concluded Jim would need to trade off weekends with his Dad and time at home. There was no easy solution to be found as attending to one's family and caring for one's dying father are both noble callings. The Paulsons simply found their way to a better place—one each of them could see as good enough—in a difficult situation.

Navigating to this better place was possible because the Paulsons saw themselves as actors in this situation, with choices they were able to make. At times, people dismiss their ability to act, attributing suffering to the will of God. Ellsberg reminds us, "the 'will of God' need not serve as a benediction over our fate; God does not 'will' that we suffer. It is, instead, the latent challenge that meets us within, or despite, every situation, the challenge to respond in a way that bears witness to love, to justice, to the truth."[10] As Sandy and Jim Paulson *worked*—and we sensed there was work involved—through the tension of competing goods, attempting to draw on a finite amount of time, they sought a response that could better bear witness to the love they held for one another.

One woman told us of her role as the eldest among her siblings; they looked to her for guidance in dealing with their mother's increasing dementia symptoms. Ultimately it was determined her mother needed to be settled in a nursing home. And this eldest daughter was retired which meant she had the most time available. There was no reward for the significant time she spent with her ailing mother. "I felt like I was the scapegoat really because [in my mother's eyes] everything that went wrong was my fault." She pause and took a deep breath. "And I forgave her, but it hurt. It hurt really deeply."

Another woman talked about her mother's death and what it meant for their family that at the time included four young children: "[My husband] would take the kids to the farm and then he would come home, get them ready for bed, put them all to bed. Then I would go to the hospital and stay there until ten or midnight when she was really bad. That was shortly before she passed away. So that was a really stressful time for us. We did what we had to do."

This "doing what you have to do" at a time of pain and suffering evokes the witness of Jesuit Fr. Walter Ciszek who, Ellsberg tells us, was imprisoned for twenty-three years in the Soviet gulag. Ciszek wrote, "For each of us, salvation means no more and no less than taking up daily the same cross of Christ, accepting each day what it brings as the will of God, offering back to God each morning all the joys, works, and sufferings of that day."[11]

In the face of a mother's death, this couple did what they had to do, welcoming the joy, work, and suffering each day brought. This is a choice one is able to make in the face of the suffering that life imposes, the choice to enter in and do what one must. In classic Christian terms we might refer to such entering in as bearing one's cross. In his treatment of suffering, Ellsberg references the timeless classic *The Imitation of Christ* in which Thomas à Kempis instructs: "The cross always stands ready, and everywhere awaits you. . . . If you bear the cross willingly it will bear you and lead you to your desired goal, where pain shall be no more. . . . If you bear the cross unwillingly, you make it a burden and load yourself more heavily; but you must needs bear it. If you cast away one cross, you will certainly find another, and perhaps a heavier."[12]

One couple shared the story of a weighty cross as they told us in somber terms how they eventually learned that their children had been repeatedly molested by a relative. We heard their story of shock and outrage, courageous confrontation of the perpetrator, denial by his spouse, and the risk of permanently severed relationships in the extended family. We learned of their complete belief in and support for their children, and the devastation they felt for not having realized, having truly not seen what later became evident as signs of a deep problem. And of course we heard of the importance of counseling for the individual children and for the family as a whole. These children are now grown, married happily, and raising their own beautiful families. But their parents tell the story as though it happened yesterday, and they call to mind the importance of a counselor who spoke hope to them with conviction: "I can tell you have a very strong family and you will get through this." That is the meaning they take from this experience: no silver lining, no imposition from God, but the deep affirmation that they are a strong family that meets suffering and indeed moves through it.

A Paschal View of Suffering: A Witness of the Body of Christ

As theologian Richard R. Gaillardetz describes, a Christian understanding of the paschal mystery is derived from the Hebrew experience of Passover or Pasch. In chapter 12 of the Book of Exodus, God instructs Moses to have his people mark their doorways with blood so that on the night they eat the Passover lamb, when the firstborn of every household is to be struck down, those homes with blood on the lintel will be passed over and no harm will come to their children.

This is part of the larger narrative "in which God delivered the Israelites from slavery into freedom."[13] Christians view Christ as the new paschal lamb who passes through death to new life. But Gaillardetz notes that Christians should look not only at the final events of the life of Christ as paschal in nature. "The central challenge of Christian life is to internalize and make the spiritual rhythm of life-death-life our own."[14]

It is easy to understand moments of suffering in our lives as experiences of death. But what we saw time and again in the couples we met was an understanding of suffering that walked in step with new life. Ellsberg notes that for the saints, suffering "did not simply strip away their illusions but also opened up new possibilities and quickened their sensitivity to the presence of grace. Suffering, in this sense, could be a merciful friend and a profound spiritual guide."[15] Our couples evidenced such saintly ability, an attentiveness to grace in the presence of suffering. We witnessed this ability poignantly when couples spoke of the suffering or death of a child.

One parish community was deeply impacted by the death of a teen at the hand of another young parishioner. New to this church community at the time, a woman told us, "I really felt a part of that story in a way that was life changing. You know, there's a witness of the Body of Christ at this parish."

A witness of the Body of Christ—as she and others told us the story of this tragic time in their parish community, their descriptions were filled with testimony to life and death . . . one young life ended, another inalterably changed, two families grieving losses of sons, and a church community gathering around all the hurt in a spirit of love and forgiveness. Those in the room gave shape to the story, with different people chiming in, making it one collective narrative, that reminded us of the familiar story of the Road to Emmaus from Luke 24. In this passage, two followers of Jesus are walking the road and discussing all that happened in the recent days of the suffering and death of Jesus. The risen Christ joins them in their walk, listens to their stories, and interprets them in light of Scripture. The two finally recognize Jesus when they break bread together.

Some years later, the parish members we met still walk the "road to Emmaus," speaking all they have known about suffering and love, and encountering Christ again as they tell the stories and gather at table.

Several couples we met experienced the death of their own child. It was midway through pregnancy when Brendan and Sarah Ruffalo learned their first child had a heart defect. Doctors prepared them for the series of surgeries and activity limitations that could mark this child's life. What they were not prepared for was the reality that their son, their firstborn, would in fact live only five days after his birth.[16] His short life and death understandably sent the young couple into a deep experience of grief, grief they each navigated differently and that caused friction between them. As Sarah tells the story, we hear the sadness, but we also recognize that she tells a resurrection story, one that believes in new life: "But then again you make it through. And I think that we were much stronger together. You kind of feel like you fought a war together and you make it through. And then you have these two beautiful healthy children that I would hope I would have been grateful for anyway, but you are so much more grateful for. . . . And so I feel like our first baby's life gave us a lot of purpose. He has added to the meaning of our lives and the meaning of our children."

To be sure, the Ruffalos wish their son had survived. But despite his death, that permanently marks the life of their family, they have passed over to a place of depth and meaning; as people who know dying, they are profoundly grateful for the experience of living.

When Jeff and Laura Rader's first pregnancy ended in miscarriage, Laura quickly returned to work only to realize she could not make it through the day. A kind coworker saw her grief and suggested she might not be ready to be back yet. So Laura called Jeff, who was able to break away from work at lunch, and the two of them spent the rest of the day together. "We sat over lunch together and said, 'Okay, why did this happen to us?' But maybe that's not the most important question. The question is: 'How do we go on from here?'"

"Why did this happen to us?" This is a fair question, an honest question. One imagines the Raders could have reviewed the months of the pregnancy and checked off all the guidelines they followed. Perhaps, with a tinge of bitterness, they might have called to mind others who were able to deliver a healthy baby despite the apparent recklessness with which they moved through pregnancy. But that is not what they discussed, according to Laura: "We decided that the good that could come out of it is that we could grow more compassionate with people who go through this experience in their own way . . . we thought that would help us to grow in understanding and compassion so we could help other people. . . . " Growing through suffering into deeper compassion—this is resurrection vision. This is a view on the world that understands that death is real and painful, but that it calls us to generosity and care.

Jack and Gretchen Baker also experienced the death of a child. They described the challenge it was, still in their first year of marriage, to lose their daughter in childbirth. Gretchen explained, "And the challenges of life kind of slap you in the face. Up until then we were still living a life of young people that were in control. You know, the youth have that, they have no fear because they think they are in control." She reflected on the way this experience helped her and Jack realize their limitations, enabling them to turn more fully to God. Gretchen concluded, "You can go no place else but to reach to God."

Their grief—deep, prolonged, and distinct for each of them—held the potential to pull them apart. They knew they were committed to each other, but as a couple both young and newly married, the fact that they wore grief distinctly and needed different things to move through it was a deep challenge. Eventually they found their way to a grief support group for parents, and they remained in it for years. Initially it was what helped them move toward wholeness. In turn, they learned to help others and eventually became leaders of the group. Gretchen explains their abiding commitment to help others in their grief: "It was mostly, the fact is, that God helps you heal when you start helping others. And we realized that very early on, that we were gaining more from this than anyone else. And healing truly does come when you can give of love in a different way. Cause it feels like love is ripped out of your heart, and God's teaching you how to love and give love, and there's nothing more beautiful to help you heal than that."

"God is teaching you how to love." Not by capriciously throwing pain into your path, but by showing you a way through pain into deeper love. The mystery of Christ who lives, suffers, dies, and lives again is the mystery to which we are called as Christians. We will never evade suffering, but we are called to live so that death cannot claim the final word. As Robert Ellsberg writes, "We can repeat what the saints learned from experience. By identifying their suffering with the cross of Christ, they found more than consolation; they found a way to transfigure their suffering, binding themselves more intimately to the love of God and to more compassionate union with their neighbors."[17]

Supporting One Another: I Couldn't Do This . . .

Time and again we saw in the couples we met the deepening of care and compassion as a fruit of suffering. They made it through because they found a way to support one another, and because they opened themselves to the support of their communities.

Jeff and Laura Rader built their first home together. We do not mean they met the very real challenges of selecting every paint color and finish for a contractor to utilize. We mean they *built* it, the two of them, with one circular saw and years of nights and weekends spent on the land they purchased. At one point in the process, when the roof was about to go up, a storm the insurance company claimed did not cross their land collapsed all the work they had completed. Laura speaks of meeting Jeff after hours at his place of work, with a six-pack in hand. "I got him a pack of beer. 'We can do this again.' He was just a frazzle with all the work he had been doing physically and emotionally. He had so much wanted to get that framing behind him, you know. Yeah, that was hard—we made it through that." The damage was devastating to them both, but in this moment Laura understood that Jeff was in the more vulnerable place, so she met his vulnerability with frothy kindness and reassurance, *we can do this again*. Happily, they were able to do it again, living still in the house that love built.

Many couples spoke of supporting one another in stressful times and moments of hardship. Christine Kozak reflected on the impact of her father-in-law's death early in their marriage. It was one of their first experiences of death, and it was the death of a man she and her husband both loved dearly. And so the grieving was difficult. But in it they learned how to share their feelings with one another. Addressing her husband, Christine said, "I know it helped you to talk about things more." Turning to us she continued, "I mean, he really got to that point where he was able to talk more and be more open. He is one of the rare men who is able to talk about his feelings and just comfortably talk about it, and a lot of guys don't do that. You know, they shut down."

In the midst of the great hardship of losing a father too soon, this couple gained a skill that served them throughout marriage—the ability to share honestly with one another what they are feeling so that they can support each other well.

Kevin and Lisa Landwehr spoke of the profound loss they experienced when one of their five children took his life. The two looked at one another somberly as Lisa explained, "After our son passed away (he committed suicide so it was a very difficult time for both of us), I quickly learned that [we] grieve differently. But we also learned that we share common grief. We knew we needed to support each other to get through it."

Supporting one another became a focal point as they continued the journey of marriage and parenthood, marked by the painful loss of their son. Lisa notes their determination to get through this tragedy together: "We made up our minds early that we were not going to be another statistic like some other families . . . that was a tough time. That was a tough time." With commitment and patience they did get through it, and many years later their relationship is clearly filled with joy and caring.

Jake and Susan Wrede were among the younger couples we met, but suffering had not eluded them. One of their daughters had successfully battled cancer, and Susan was in the midst of her own cancer journey when we met her. Recalling the days and weeks spent in the hospital with their young child, Jake looked at his wife, "We kind of took turns in comforting each other. The first few days it was [a lot of] the doctor coming in and either you would be crying and I would be comforting you or there were times where I was the one tearing up and you were comforting me."

Matthew and Margaret Murphy similarly described taking turns with need and support when facing a difficult time with a child. Matthew shook his head as he recalled, "I mistakenly thought, *You know, if we can just get them through the teenage years . . .* but it's been much harder as young adults, particularly this past year." As their children faced struggles with physical and mental health, Matthew continued, "It was very painful—it was the first time in our marriage when I wasn't sure what to do. Talk about leaning on each other. And usually one of us is the strong one. We both literally were holding each other up."

This mutual care for one another in a time of deep fear and sadness is something we heard couples speak of time and again. They could not avoid difficulties, but they moved through them with tremendous care for one another.

In this exchange between Pat and Carol Landry, we see the profound importance of the spouses supporting one another. Pat and Carol raised two fine sons, both out of college, and take great pride in them both. In recent times, the younger of the two sons has experienced serious difficulties. The couple opened up and allowed us to hear what that has meant for them:

> Carol: I think you feel alone because maybe people don't know what to do or how to help you. And we don't even know what we need.
>
> Pat: It's so foreign. Our son is getting in trouble . . .
>
> Carol: We just learned this year he's an alcoholic.
>
> Pat: Very serious.
>
> Carol: He has some DUIs and legal troubles and is currently living with us. It's just—we're doing everything we're supposed to but . . .
>
> Pat: the future . . .
>
> Carol: Alcoholism is a 50/50 chance that you're going to be okay or you're not going to be okay. [T]his is a kid who was a straight-A student, did everything right his whole life and in college. Never screwed up, never made mistakes. Wonderful friend, very respectful. Got a job, self-supporting. Better job, more self-supporting.
>
> Pat: [I]t's really hard. Our life is completely changed. Everything is different and the future, we don't know what it is going to look like . . .
>
> Carol: But we're learning.
>
> Pat: But our relationship . . . I don't know how we'd do it. I couldn't do this . . .
>
> Carol: I couldn't do this.
>
> Pat: without Carol . . . the only thing I'm pretty—I'm more than pretty—I'm confident that we'll make it together because I think we're more bonded now than we've ever been . . . I think these challenges really bring us together.
>
> Carol: I'm going to cry!

And Carol did begin to cry softly, dabbing away the tears. A bit later in the conversation, Pat spoke about getting together with colleagues to share with them what was going on in his family life. He wanted them to understand why he might not seem fully on his A-game, how a deadline might be missed or he might appear distracted in a staff meeting. He describes their reaction:

> Pat: I called a meeting of our department to explain what I was going through because I knew I was going to be a little wacky. They knew—when I called the meeting, they knew something was up. When I told them the story, my colleagues breathed a sigh of relief and said, "Oh, we thought maybe you were ill!" And I said, "Listen, an illness is nothing! This is so much worse than that!"
>
> Carol: And it's fascinating how this stuff . . . in any moment your world could turn any way! I don't know . . . I thought I lived in [my town] but apparently I live on Neptune and I didn't buy a ticket! How does that happen? That's where humor helps because you sit next to each other sometimes and say, "Are we alive?"

Pat and Carol laugh together again. They sit closely, hands clasped when their story touches on difficult truths, and their laughter as well their head-shaking are nearly always synchronized. We *see* them moving through this hardship together. And in Carol's final comment, we glimpse the importance of humor as marriages navigate difficult times. Indeed, among those we surveyed, 71 percent claimed a sense of humor was extremely important in a successful marriage. Eighty percent indicated patience was extremely important, and 67 percent indicated hope is extremely important.[18]

Obviously, these characteristics can be tapped in good times and in bad, in sickness and in health, but it is in the times of difficulty that the couples feel the need for humor, patience, and hope most deeply. These are the times that call them to reach for and out to one another, attending to each other with great care as they navigate suffering.

An Expanded Circle of Support: We Were Just So Held

Support for one another is clearly important to any couple experiencing suffering, but the circle of support at difficult times is often more expansive. We asked the couples we surveyed about the places they found support in times of stress or struggle. Ninety percent said their family and friends played an important role in these moments, and 85 percent indicated they looked to their church community for support in difficult times.[19]

Mike and Sophia Vandenbusch had followed work to a state hundreds of miles from both of their homes. Shortly before the birth of their second child, Mike was transferred back home, and due to the quickness of the change, the couple temporarily moved in with Sophia's parents. In retrospect this was a blessing because, not long after, Sophia miscarried. "So when we lost the baby, we were living around all of our family. We had everyone here. And I can't even imagine how much more difficult it would have been had we been alone, but we had everybody here with us."

The support of those who knew and loved them best held them through a time of tremendous grief. Friends and family gathered round with care and gave them space to move through grieving in the time they needed. Sophia reflected, "You go through that period where you think life will be horrible forever and then all of a sudden, it just isn't." In that period when life seems permanently horrible, a vibrant circle of support is critically important.

We heard many stories of times when the circle of care and support expanded beyond immediate family and closest friends, to parish communities responding to the call to care for any who are vulnerable or hurting. Frank and Kelly Brown appear to this day to be a young and fit couple. But that did not stop cancer from entering their lives, and the role of their parish family in walking that difficult road with them is clear to Kelly. "We were just so held and so fed literally and spiritually through that whole time, with two little boys and someone going through chemo—nine weeks of chemo—to just be so cared for. I can't even imagine being any other place because now this community is just so important to us." They are indebted, and in turn deeply committed, to their parish family, the community that held them through a frightening time.

Susan Wisniewski speaks of a similar sort of road to parish commitment for her and husband Tim, supported on the difficult road through the sickness and death of their daughter. "[I]t really shifted in my heart when our daughter Melissa got sick. And this, as well as all our other communities, just stepped forward, and we felt like, I think I can say this for both of us . . . " She and Tim exchange glances and nod to one another in affirmation, "[T]hat's when we felt like our toes were barely brushing the ground. We were being carried through our whole journey and through and beyond the time she died."

She goes on to explain that they have since moved to another part of town, making participation in this parish no longer geographically convenient. But it remains their parish, and one in which they are now more deeply involved, "We had such a great deep sense of gratitude and belonging that even though we live [in another part of town], I can't even imagine walking away from here. And we continue to find opportunities to give back to families that are in need at any point in a kind of counter-bank. You can bake a casserole [and] you can put it into a central depository."

This "central depository" of compassion and kindness is a wonderful image for parish families. People make deposits not knowing if they will ever need to draw, in fact hoping they never will, but when hardship comes, the coffers of caring are full and available. How often do we dismiss such efforts, thinking we have done little as we drop off a pan of lasagna and a tray of lemon bars? In conversation with fellow parishioners, Matthew Murphy allowed us to glimpse what it can mean to be on the receiving end of such kindness:

> I'll never forget: when [our daughter] was in the hospital last fall, I was traumatized; I lost ten pounds in a matter of a few weeks. And we were taking turns going down to see her in the hospital. And I came home . . . and there was a cooler on the doorstep full of meals that you all provided . . . . We had given to the meals ministry over the years but never had been recipients. I can remember, I told Margaret this, that I was home all alone. . . . And I was sitting there eating this meatloaf, that [a parishioner] had left, and I just started to cry. Because I had this experience of being fed.

In chapter 21 of the Gospel of John, Peter is told that if he loves the Lord, he will demonstrate this love by feeding his sheep. Each of us is called to respond to the deep hungers in the world. In this moment, Matthew—a caring father and involved community and parish member—understood the profound impact of "being fed."

One woman spoke with deep appreciation of the love she felt from her parish community when her husband underwent open-heart surgery. She described sitting in the very tense waiting area wrapped in a prayer shawl a parish group had given her, and feeling she was being held by the prayers of so many parishioners.

This extension of care is reflected in the story of Mark and Jeanne Carter, sought out by others in their parish when it became widely known their son Charlie is gay. Parishioners, some elderly, finally felt they could admit to someone that their own child was gay or lesbian. Thinking both of the people who supported them and of those they in turn supported, Mark concludes, "People do want to talk. They want to be supportive. Be loving."

People do want to be supportive, loving. Our parishes do best when they make spaces for that love to be extended to those members who are suffering.

In his book *God, Medicine and Suffering*, theologian Stanley Hauerwas cautions against theological attempts to explain evil or suffering, instead offering a book that attempts to explain "why we cannot afford to give ourselves explanations for evil when what is required is a community capable of absorbing our grief."[20] Hauerwas utilizes the death of a child as the focal point for his discussion, for surely this is among the least *explainable* forms of suffering. His book begins with a quotation from Nicholas Wolterstorff's work *Lament for a Son*, and Hauerwas returns to this text for the final words in his treatise on suffering: "If you think your task as comforter is to tell me that really, all things considered, it's not so bad, you do not sit with me in my grief but place yourself off in the distance away from me. Over there, you are of no help. What I need to hear from you is that you recognize how painful it is. I need to hear from you that you are with me in my desperation. To comfort me, you have to come close. Come sit beside me on my mourning bench."[21]

Suffering reveals our vulnerability and in that revelation we naturally seek ways we can give explanations of meaning or attempt to do something about it. We want a way to exert reason or control in a place of helplessness. But as Hauerwas instructs, suffering's call is perhaps less about doing than receiving, opening up, risking vulnerability, and allowing for our spouse and others to offer care and support. That is what the Landrys had to do. When asked what times of trouble have meant to them, Carol tells us, "I can give a one-word answer to your question: gratitude. We've had some horrible stuff. We're in the middle of some horrible stuff right now . . . we've had so much love from people around us. The times that we've found ourselves crying were out of gratitude and not sorrow." Truly, gratitude can be the final word when someone knows how to sit beside you in your suffering.

6

"Nobody's Leaving"

The Power and Path of Fidelity

"Fidelity requires us not only not to end or walk out of loving relationships but more importantly to defend and sustain them."[1] This assertion, made by Catholic ethicist James Keenan, captures the essence of fidelity, or faithfulness. The virtue of fidelity demands that particular, interpersonal relationships—such as relationships with friends, family members, and married partners—be *defended* and *sustained*. Moreover, from a Catholic perspective, Keenan argues that fidelity ought to be informed by mercy.

In chapter 4, we defined mercy from a Christian perspective, but it is nevertheless worth pondering Keenan's powerful definition of mercy here—that is, mercy is "the willingness to enter into the chaos of another so as to respond to their need."[2] In our examination of service and hospitality, we thought about mercy primarily as it applies to more general relationships. Here, we will consider what faithfulness looks like in the married relationship, a faithfulness that includes a willingness to enter into the chaos of one's spouse and the chaos of shared life. We begin by considering the implications of promising fidelity in marriage from a theological perspective.

When a couple participates in the sacrament of matrimony in the Catholic tradition, they promise a lifetime of fidelity to one another, consenting to "be true" to one another in "good times and in bad, in sickness and in health." They pledge to "love and honor" each other "all the days" of their lives.[3] From that moment on, they are bound by their promise—to God and to each other—and their commitment is symbolized by the exchange of rings.

In *Personal Commitments*, theologian Margaret Farley explains the meaning of the making of vows and exchange of rings in the marriage ceremony. Farley notes that a vow or pledge is different from a *prediction*, which is a judgment about a future over which a person is not necessarily responsible (for example, a meteorologist makes a prediction about weather, but cannot control the weather and thus is not held responsible if it rains rather than snows).

A vow is also different from a *resolution*, which is an obligation only to oneself (for example, I may resolve to exercise more often, and can hold myself responsible for following through or not, but I am responsible only to myself regarding that resolution—thank goodness). In contrast, when I give my word to another person by proclaiming vows, I "give the other person a claim over me, that I will perform the action to which I have committed myself . . . as a pledge . . . . It claims my faithfulness, my constancy, not just because I have spoken it to myself, but because it now calls to me from the other person who has received it."[4]

The wedding rings "concretize" the vows that are exchanged. The rings, rather than simply being "given away," somehow belong to both partners because they signify the word that each spouse has given to the other and to which each remains bound.[5]

The marriage commitment "entails a new relation in the present[6]—a relation of binding and being-bound, giving and being-claimed. But commitment also points to the future. The whole reason for the present 'obligating' is to try to influence the future, to try to commit ourselves to do the actions we intend and promise."[7] By pledging unconditional (in good times and bad, until death do we part) love and fidelity in the wedding liturgy, we *assure* our spouse and the community that we will be consistent and we "*strengthen* ourselves for fulfilling our present intentions in an otherwise uncertain future."[8]

We obligate ourselves to love and honor our beloved now and into the future, understanding that he or she will inevitably change, that our relationship will change, and that faithfulness must be lived in ever-changing circumstances. Once vows and rings are exchanged, spouses are bound to one another and have a claim over each other; future choices are henceforth choices of either *fidelity* or *betrayal*.[9]

Couples that we interviewed spoke pointedly about the meaning of their vows, which ground their fidelity to one another. In the midst of discussing a particularly challenging period of his marriage, Jim Donlan said: "When did it become an option that you could just leave? Never. I mean, we all stood up on an altar in front of our friends and God and everybody. Those vows are not a multiple choice. It isn't 'for better or worse, for richer or poorer: yes, no, yes, no.' It is 'yes' to all of it. So it isn't an option."

Jim's firm belief that leaving his marriage "isn't an option" in light of vows exchanged was affirmed again and again by our interviewees, with many people using that very language: "divorce is not an option." One woman put it this way, "When I married my husband, I took an oath under God. And that getting divorced is against that oath. I took an oath in front of the church and in front of God that he would be my husband until the end of my life, until death do us part. And that is first and foremost."

One particularly helpful discussion about marital fidelity developed in a focus group. The exchange between two couples—Todd and Jenny Phillips, and Tim and Donna Erikson—begins with a comment from Todd, who is reflecting on the early days of his thirty-two-year marriage to Jenny, when they had two small children and money was tight:

Todd: [We were] just struggling and struggling and struggling. And I think it made us a lot closer. We struggled together and worked through it and stayed together. While other people around us were getting divorced and stuff, we just kept . . .

Jenny: kept doing it.

Todd: We worked through those hard times and waited for the good times to come. We just didn't give up on each other.

Jenny: We didn't give up on each other. We talked through things. We would say, "What's the best plan? What can we do? How can we balance this?"

Todd: "What can we do without?"

Jenny: Yeah, "What can we do without? Let's not be selfish about anything. Just: What do we need for the family or the household to get by?" And it was always going to church, always keeping our faith. Bringing the kids to church . . .

Tim: I don't know where it came from, but it just wasn't an option, that option of "Well, okay we're struggling, I could leave."

Donna: We never would have thought that! No. It never crossed my mind.

Jenny: It never crossed my mind either. It was a sacrament. We did it before God and before our family and it was important. *We're in it together. Let's make it work.*

Donna: Now [thirty-two years later] we have the pact, because we're older and we do stupid things and lose things, and we say, "All right, let's shake on this. Nobody's leaving! [Laughter from the group.] No matter what happens from here on out! Nobody's leaving!"

Donna's last comment, while humorous, points to the changing responsibilities of faithfulness over time. Fidelity takes different shapes. How a
couple "makes it work" alters, depending upon age and circumstance. In
the conversation above, Todd and Jenny reflect on the challenges of staying
committed when raising children as young parents without financial security,
while Donna hints at what fidelity looks like when couples age. In other
conversations, spouses described fidelity as learning to trust and be faithful
while regularly separated from each other due to work and travel. Others
spoke of the intense demands of faithfulness to a partner after losing a child
or parent, or when one spouse is ill or depressed. And the list goes on, because
life goes on, and each day calls married couples to practice fidelity anew.

Frank Brown highlights the daily and changing nature of fidelity, saying,
"It's like each day when you wake up, it's like you get married again; you
have to choose each other each day. So, it's kind of like, we don't say it out
loud. . . ." His wife Kelly chimed in, "There have been times when we
have, though! We've needed to." Frank explained, "You kind of wake up in
the morning and roll over and say, 'I choose you.' I mean again. No matter
what." Kelly said, "I would name that value faithfulness, a Christian value.
Faithfulness means, 'Yeah, I say yes to this, I choose this, I believe this no
matter what comes."

Donna Erikson also highlights the importance of daily choice in loving
another over a lifetime: "Love is a choice that we make every day. You know,
every day you make that choice: I am going to love that person." For these
married persons, faithfulness looks like being determined each day—to
choose to love and be faithful to one's spouse.

A few couples used the language of covenant when discussing their vows
and responsibilities to be faithful to one another and to God. For example,
Angie Smith said, "We took a vow. It was the two of us and God in this
covenant relationship. It's not just us. This is our covenant with God," and
thus unbreakable.

The Catholic tradition has drawn extensively on covenant imagery to
argue that marriage is *indissoluble*—in other words, sacramental marriage
between two baptized Christian cannot be dissolved. Symbolically, once the
spouses have become "one body" in marriage, they cannot be broken apart.
Covenant imagery for marriage appears in both the Hebrew Scriptures and
in the New Testament. In the Hebrew Scriptures, prophets such as Hosea,
Jeremiah, and Ezekial compare the covenant between married partners to the
covenant that exists between God (YHWH) and the people of Israel. God's
covenant fidelity becomes the model for marital fidelity—just as God is

faithful to the people despite their inadequacies and betrayals, spouses should likewise be faithful to one another. In "Marriage in the Bible," theologian Michael Lawler notes that "[God's] covenant fidelity becomes a characteristic to be imitated, a challenge to be accepted, in every Jewish marriage."[10]

In the New Testament, covenant imagery shifts from YHWH-Israel to Christ-church. In turn, the unbreakable covenant between Christ and the church becomes a model for Christian covenantal marriage. Chapter 5 from the Letter to the Ephesians makes the comparison clear: "Husbands, love your wives, just as Christ loved the church and gave himself up for her. . . . For this reason, a man shall leave his father and mother and be joined to his wife, and the two shall become one flesh. This is a great mystery, and I am applying it to Christ and the church" (Eph 5:25, 31–32). Lawler explains that, "the union between Christ and the Church provides an ideal model for human marriage and for the mutual conduct of the spouses within it."[11] Just as Christ "gives himself up" for the church, serves the church, and loves the church "steadfastly and faithfully," so spouses are called to mutually give way to one another, serve one another, and be steadfastly faithful to one another in their marital covenant.[12]

Farley argues, "[I]t is necessary to remember that both the Hebrew and Christian scriptures portray overall a God whose desire is a relationship with human persons, whose commitment is renewed again and again, and who in fact professes often to love with an unconditional love. The story of the Covenant is ultimately a story of a God who does not withdraw divine promises or presence, despite every provocation."[13] Therefore, God's covenantal relationship is a powerful ideal for the married relationship in which—ideally—commitment is renewed again and again, and promises of unconditional love are not withdrawn, no matter the provocation. In Kelly Brown's words: Daily, "I say yes to this, I choose this, I believe this *no matter what comes.*"

In light of Scripture—particularly the covenantal imagery in the New Testament—Lawler makes an important statement about indissolubility: "Christian marriage is indissoluble because Christian love is steadfast and faithful. Indissolubility is a quality of Christian marriage because it is, first, a quality of Christian love."[14] Theologian Richard Gaillardetz argues that, if marital love only exists imperfectly (because there is still room for growth) on a wedding day, then indissolubility also only exists imperfectly. Therefore, "marital love, as mutual giving-way, as mutual service, as mutual fidelity, as mainspring of indissoluble community, is not a given in a Christian marriage but *a task to be undertaken.*"[15] For spouses, being unconditionally faithful and loving, forming an unbreakable personal union, is not something that magically happens on one's wedding day. It is not simply a given once vows are exchanged. Instead, it is "a task to be undertaken" throughout one's marriage. In Lawler's words, "permanence is not a static . . . quality of a marriage, but a dynamic, living quality of human love on which marriage, both human and Christian, thrives."[16]

Conflict, Communication, and Fidelity: It's Not Easy to Do!

Indeed, being a faithful spouse for a lifetime is a task and an achievement, and sometimes it is more difficult than others. "Fidelity means faithfulness through living the vows of marriage in sickness and in health and until death do us part. You know the times when the marriage gets challenged, when difficult or bad things happen . . . that's where those vows really come into play," Steve Miller told us. One of those difficult times in Steve's twenty-six-year marriage was when his wife, Barbara, was being treated for advanced cancer. Steve claimed that "living through that experience"—giving each other emotional and spiritual support, making decisions jointly about Barbara's treatment, traveling together for her medical care, nursing her during her illness—was "living fidelity."

Indeed, in the Millers' attentive love and support for one another throughout Barbara's battle with cancer (surely an example of chaos), we see lived fidelity informed by mercy. In chapter 5, we shared many stories of how couples practice fidelity in the face of suffering. In this section, we will focus specifically on interpersonal conflict in marriage, which—like suffering—is inevitable and provides challenges during which marital vows to love faithfully "really come into play." We will see that when couples disagree and are angry at each other, they nevertheless can find ways to be faithful—that is, to defend and sustain their relationship.

Anne Marie Donlan believes that seeing a situation from your spouse's perspective is an important method for solving conflict in marriage; she tries to do this on a regular basis, though it can be difficult. She told us about the tense time period before one of their sons, Paul, left home to go into the military, an unexpected decision, "completely out of the blue." The decision had a particularly powerful effect on Jim, who is typically the less emotional of the married couple. Anne Marie said:

> I will always look at the other person's point of view—where will he be coming from? What is his personality? And how is he looking at this situation? And why is it making him so angry or sad or whatever it is . . . like right before Paul went. [Anne Marie begins to

cry while reflecting back. She looks at her husband, Jim.] You were angry a lot. You were angry. And I think it was a man's version of not knowing how to express himself. That made me angry because I'm like, *we only have this much time before he goes away so don't spend it angry!* So I got kind of angry with him. So that was a conflict for us. He would get upset with me, "Why are you blaming me?" And I was like, "Why are you being so angry?" And finally I just had to sit down and think: *What is driving that anger for him? It's not anger. It's sadness . . .* You have to know somebody a long time and put those pieces together and try to be compassionate, you know, from that perspective. And it's not easy to do!

Anne Marie prayed. Her prayer was, "God, help. Show me how to help him. Tell me how to help him. Tell me what to say. How do I comfort him?" She was trying to keep her anger and frustration under control so that their children would not see that she and Jim were fighting during an already strained time at home. So she took Jim out to the garage, in private, and they "had a little bit of a conversation." That conversation allowed them to air their concerns and feelings and begin to mend, as a couple and as concerned parents. With Anne Marie's help, Jim came to understand and bear with his feelings of sadness at the prospect of "the whole empty nest thing," that he described as "shockingly hard for me."

In retrospect, they both spoke articulately about their feelings related to their son's decision to enter the military and leave home, but it is clear that the process of sorting out those feelings and expressing them in healthy ways was a complicated one. Jim expressed gratitude for his wife who "forced [him] to look at it differently than what I was going through" and to see more clearly how she and their children were being affected as well. Anne Marie did admirable emotional work in the midst of a stressful conflict. She tried to dig underneath her husband's anger to get at its root, and eventually found sadness. Anne Marie said, "It definitely helps, I think, trying to look at how your spouse is looking at it, the perspective that they are coming from definitely helps. I feel that doesn't happen overnight. That's a process."

She worked to see Jim compassionately in the midst of her frustration, and she prayed about how to effectively reach out to him and meet his needs; in our minds, this demonstrates the kind of giving-way and service that ought to mark covenantal love. "Knowing [her husband] a long time" and praying helped Anne Marie better understand his point of view and identify that he needed to be comforted. Ultimately, she helped them both move toward healing by "creating a space" to talk through their feelings. In this case, it happened to be a garage!

A number of the spouses we spoke to, like Anne Marie, came to understand over the course of their marriage that anger may be displaced. One wife admits that, after work, her husband is "the first one to get yelled at for everything everyone dumps onto me all day long . . . I walk in the door and it's all his fault, whatever it was. He's always pretty good about that." Her husband responded, "I think you have to recognize when someone is yelling at you, often times they are yelling at the situation, but they are yelling at you. It's directed at you, but it's not personal. You have to recognize that."

A spouse might simply be venting frustration with a most-trusted person (one's spouse) in a safe place (at home), believing that their partner will meet that venting with understanding and generosity, hoping that the spouse will not take it personally but rather listen compassionately. Al Kozak said, "Over the years, I've learned that sometimes she might just want to vent. She doesn't want me to solve her issue, and I don't want her to solve my issue. Just sit there, or lie there, and I want to tell you what's on my mind, get it out of me, and I can move on, and not always say you've gotta fix it. Over the years I've had to really work at listening. Sometimes at the end, I'll ask, 'So do you want me to suggest [a solution]? Or fix it?' And she'll be like, 'Nope. I just want you to listen.'"

One husband insightfully noted that conflict in marriage often occurs "when one of us is stressed for whatever reason." [Others in the focus group nodded in agreement.] He explained, "I mean, it could be you haven't eaten all day long or you're running on empty on sleep or it's just stressful because of whatever is going on. And those are the things that lead up to that little whatever-it-is becoming that blowup moment."

In light of this, while it may be tempting to "take the bait" and respond in anger to a spouse's mood or words, sometimes what is required is practicing patience, calmly listening, giving a hug, or maybe making a sandwich. We know from experience: a snack and some sympathy can go a surprisingly long way toward de-escalating conflict! Long term, of course, spouses have a responsibility to take good care of themselves insofar as they are able—to get enough sleep, to eat well, to get regular exercise—in order to be healthy in mind and body and thus more easily manage anger and frustration. But patience and gentleness with one another in the midst of day-to-day ups and downs is crucial over the long haul.

Spouses in our study also emphasized the necessity of patience and understanding when dealing with different styles of communication within marriage.[17] For instance, Margaret Murphy quickly discovered that her husband Matthew "tends to want to retreat" during conflict, whereas her tendency is to attack head on—to pursue a discussion immediately "because I want to get it over now! I want to be done." She says that, while she is "not always great at it," she tries to honor her husband's need to process matters. Over the course of their marriage, Margaret has developed the understanding that their different personality types as well as their different upbringings affect the ways that they each "process and deal with things." This knowledge has allowed her to be more "lovingly understanding" of her husband, rather than growing frustrated when he does not respond to things exactly as she might.

Spouses who, like Margaret and Matthew, have dissimilar communication styles have needed to develop strategies for solving conflict that accommodate those different styles. One husband told us—for example—that he lets his wife vocalize her point of view right away, because that is her preference and need, while she allows him "to sit and churn things through a little more," because that is his preference and need; eventually they are able to come together to sort out the issue at hand. It took some years, however, to establish that method of dealing with conflict, and the husband told us how desperately he wishes he would have known the importance of accommodating their differences at the beginning of their relationship: "I wish someone would have told me that!"

Sometimes couples find writing to be an effective method of "churning things through" and conveying thoughts and feelings. In one case, a couple has difficulty communicating well during conflict because the husband is able to easily articulate his perspective and build arguments on the spur of the moment. On the other hand, his wife is unable to think quickly on her feet, especially when upset, and therefore feels at a significant disadvantage during a disagreement. Once the couple identified this problem, they came up with a mutually agreed upon solution. When conflict arises, if the wife feels the need to sort out her thoughts and feelings more fully, she takes time to write in a journal, after which she is more prepared for fruitful conversation. This practice seems a lovely compromise that respects each of the spouses and enhances their communication. We heard of other cases in which both partners utilize journals or write letters when they are upset, then exchange those with their spouse. They find that writing allows them to focus on the heart of their concerns rather than getting distracted by nonessential matters or getting swept up by emotion. One couple used the writing method regularly until they felt better able to stay calm and focused in face-to-face discussions, which they now prefer and do exclusively.

Katie and Bill McCarthy learned more effective strategies of communication during their years together. Katie recalled that early in their marriage, in the midst of an argument, her husband said, "I would rather not
say anything to you right now because once it comes out of my mouth, I
cannot take it back. Therefore, I will walk away from you. Because once I
tell you that . . ." Bill jumped in to finish her sentence, "I couldn't take it
back." When tempted to begin name-calling or insulting Katie out of anger,
he chose to walk away from the argument, which was new and surprising
to Katie, who grew up in a family "that liked to have big blowup fights—
scream, yell, slam doors, you know, that was the norm." Katie recognizes
the wisdom of sometimes walking away rather than attacking one's partner
in anger, claiming it is "one of the biggest lessons" Bill has ever taught
her. She believes that insulting one's spouse during an argument, saying,
"You're stupid! You're this! You're that!" is "where you could go wrong . . .
[because] once I said it, no matter if I meant it or not, I can't take it back."
Even if a person apologizes, Katie explains, "the [hurtful] words are in the
air" and the damage is done. "So therefore I would rather not say it . . . so
I think more times than not, we will depart and come back and talk later."
As noted above, she learned this tactic from Bill early in their marriage, and
they now practice it whenever necessary. Katie contends that the strategy is
much more effective than vicious arguing or continuing a heated standoff in
which each partner digs in his or her heels, believing, "I've got to be right."

Al and Christine Kozak learned a similar lesson in their twenty years of
marriage. As Christine explains, they now know that, "if we're both heated,
[if] we're both upset about something," it is best to "not say too much and
just kind of let things go . . . I think we both have a tendency to say things
we don't mean, to go off on tangents and bring things into the conversation
that are not important. And I think I have learned through the years to just
stop talking, just take a breath and not talk for a while. And it really helps,
it really does."

Likewise, Laura Rader sees the value of a temporary break from her
husband when extremely angry:

> I would say one of the things I decided about ten years ago is when
> things start to escalate when you're getting upset and pretty soon
> you're not thinking clearly, and we're raising voices—I was like,
> you know, I don't want to do that anymore. Not that I don't, but I
> wanted to work on that. One of the fruits of the Spirit is self-dis-
> cipline, so I wanted to work on that. So I decided that I was going
> to say, "You know, Honey, I'm going for a walk. I'll be back." And

it just gave us time to think, to cool down and have time to think. And to pray about it too. And sometimes I would say that, too, "I need time to think and pray about it." Or, "Let's pray about this," but we didn't always seem to want to do that [laughter] . . . So I would take an hour, an hour and a half, and then I could come back and often apologize and then we could calmly talk about what was wrong. A lot of times we were talking about surface [issues] and not the root of the problem. And when we were calm, we were able to get down to the root of it. And then we could deal with it.

What we find particularly helpful about Laura's reflection is her explicit determination to practice restraint and proper discernment when she gets angry. Keep in mind that healthy persons *should* experience anger, and inevitably *will* experience anger within any ongoing relationship. Anger is a proper and rightful response to wrongdoing and injustice. The moral question is: What do we do with that anger? Do we allow it to take over and turn into wrath? In other words, do we let it overwhelm us so that we cannot control what we do and say—thereby acting and speaking in ways that we may later (or even immediately) regret?

Interestingly, Al Kozak told us that—some years back—he asked his father-in-law what his one recommendation would be for a long marriage. His father-in-law responded: "Anger management." Al added, "He is the most mild-mannered person. He's whistling all the time. He goes, 'There will be times [marriage] will test you. You've got to find a way to channel that into something else.' He's right. He's a very wise man."

The advice given by Al's father-in-law is wise indeed. It reflects a long-standing philosophical and theological tradition that names wrath as a vice, or a "deadly sin," and therefore emphasizes the importance of channeling anger in ways that reflect and build good character and that lead to healthy relationships.

In her reflection above, Laura Rader points to self-discipline as an ideal in the face of anger. Naming self-discipline as a fruit of the Spirit, she recognizes that it is the result of grace, but also understands that it is something she needs "to work on." When Laura is angry, she practices self-discipline by paying attention to the intensity of emotions in exchanges with her husband; stepping back when the situation is escalating in order to "cool off"; reengaging when she is able to be reasonable, listen, and discuss; and ultimately cooperating to identify and address the root of the problem. For Laura, an hour or an hour-and-a-half break typically has a calming effect that helps her engage conflict more reasonably and effectively.

In other situations, the separation, or "cool off" period, may be longer. Christine Kozak indicated that sometimes when she and her partner are angry about something, they "go to bed separately" after not speaking all day. "If we're still upset the next day, at least we've had some time to kind of relax and not be angry and have so much anger when [we're] talking. That has really helped me."

In conversation with couples, we heard from some that strict adherence to the popular rule "never go to bed angry" works well in their marriage relationship. Yet, Christine's experience stands in contrast to that rule. She explains that going to bed while still angry "may mean that you are still sorting out what you want to say. You're still sorting out your feelings, and you're sorting out what they're saying [or, trying to understand your spouse's perspective]. You don't want to say things that you don't really mean or [speak] if you don't understand. You just need time to think about what you just said and what the other person has said."

Christine believes spouses need not be anxious about spending time in silence, even overnight "because you know deep down you're going to revisit this and you're going to talk about what is really important. And I think that's what happens, you [eventually] talk about the thing that is making you the most upset, and you need to focus on that. And I think when you get to the point when you're just yelling and shouting, it doesn't accomplish anything. You have to just sit and talk and be reasonable, rational."

Be reasonable. Be rational. Every long-married spouse knows the difficulty of this when angry or hurt, which is why behaving prudentially takes discipline, and sometimes demands stepping back from the situation to think and pray. In his focus group, Matthew Murphy rightly pointed out: "If we weren't human, we would just deal with the facts and take the emotion completely out of it, right? And solve the problem. But unfortunately, we don't have the ability."

True enough—we do not have the ability as humans to shut off our emotions. Nor is it healthy to do so. But, as we have seen in the testimony above, we do have the capability to manage our emotions effectively. We found that spouses are able to safely say to each other, "I need to go take a walk and pray about this"; or, "I am walking away because I don't want to say something that I regret"; or, "While I'd like to hash this out now, why don't you take some time to think about it, and we'll talk about it after dinner, or whenever you're ready," *because they trust* that they will eventually come back together with their partner. And, more than that, they are confident that when they *do* come back together, both partners will be ready and willing to resolve the conflict. As one man explained, it is the "foundation of trust and love" in a marriage that allows for significant disagreements and small "breaks" in anger. Spouses are able both to endure periods of silence, but also to (immediately or eventually) express thoughts and feelings honestly, because they trust, finally, the relationship itself will not be broken.

In light of the testimony of the couples in our study, we believe there are ways of resolving conflict that reflect and support fidelity. These include

- consistently striving to see and understand the perspective of one's spouse (this involves paying attention, listening well, and—when necessary—entering into his or her chaos);

- responding generously when one's spouse expresses anger that seems rooted in stress, hunger, or lack of sleep;

- learning and accommodating one another's differences when dealing with conflict;

- strategically keeping one's anger under control rather than allowing it to become wrath;

- taking time for prayer and reflection rather than being rash;

- and arguing well—calmly, even lovingly, expressing one's feelings and addressing the issue at hand rather than "going off" on tangents, rehashing old arguments, or saying mean or hurtful things to one's partner.

Fortunately, we heard spouses talk about getting better at resolving conflict over time, as they came to know their spouse more intimately and developed strategies for anger management and effective communication that work for both partners.

Before closing this section, allow us to briefly mention two additional practices for avoiding and responding to conflict that seem to foster fidelity: *staying connected* and *keeping a sense of humor*. Jeff and Laura Rader noticed over time that when they were getting on each other's nerves and fighting more frequently, it was usually because they had not spent enough "quality time just to relax with each other." In the day-to-day grind they had "lost their sense of humor" and were disconnected, which manifest itself in frustration with one another and misunderstanding. Consequently, whenever they sense that they have entered a period when they are quick to anger or frustration, the Raders make an effort to spend some one-on-one time together in order to renew their relationship and regain their humor.

Reconnecting and lightening up has been effective in lessening conflict in their marriage. In fact, many couples told us how humor serves to ease tension, defuse anger, and renew connectivity between partners (not to mention make life more fun!).[18]

One man, who is married thirty-nine years, wrote at the conclusion of his survey: "And, for God's sake, have a sense of humor!" Indeed, as noted in chapter 5, humor seems a necessary ingredient for a long-lasting marriage, particularly one that sustains joy in the midst of inevitable suffering and conflict.

Overall, we learned that trust in the fidelity of one's spouse—confidence that "nobody's leaving"—creates a safe environment for conflict and the expression of anger. We also learned that, while conflict has the potential to hurt married partners and even break a marriage apart, there are ways of engaging in conflict that sustain long-term fidelity, ways that show deep respect for one's spouse and for the married relationship. In the end, however, we learned from couples that controlling anger, communicating effectively, and utilizing strategies for conflict resolution only gets them so far. Fidelity cannot be sustained over the long haul without *forgiveness*. And it is to forgiveness that we now turn.

Forgiveness and Fidelity: It's a Prerequisite

"I don't know how you can have a marriage and not have forgiveness," one man said during a focus group conversation. An illustrative exchange about forgiveness followed:

> Beth Johnson: And even before it gets to forgiveness, there are a lot of faults, I'm sure I have them too, that I overlook because I love Joe. I don't focus on little things that annoy me. [Turning to her husband], I think you overlook a lot of my faults, too.
>
> Dan Vogel: I mean there's a reason that confession is one of the first sacraments: we have to be able to forgive, give forgiveness. I think in a marriage it is critical to be able to forgive and be forgiven. I mean, "forgive us as we forgive those who trespass against us." You know what I mean? If you can't do that, and you can't expect it, you're in trouble. I think that's key. It's been key for us.
>
> Beth: But it's hard for me to say I'm sorry. I don't necessarily ask for [forgiveness]. [She looks at her husband.] I think lots of times you just naturally do it.

Jocelyn King: Forgiveness is probably going on all the time. For-give ourselves, forgive our partner.

Dan: Yes. Forgive ourselves. Ask for forgiveness, from God and from your spouse. We wouldn't get very far without it.

Joe Johnson: No, like you said, it's a prerequisite. I mean, how could you. . . ?

Dan: We wouldn't even have a relationship if we were always hold-ing grudges and there was no forgiveness involved.

"We wouldn't get very far. . . . We wouldn't even have a relationship." The importance of forgiveness in long-lasting marriages cannot be underestimated.

Let us return again to God's covenant with the people as a model for marriage: without God's mercy, the covenant could not be sustained. God chooses again and again to forgive, to renew the covenant—thus enabling the relationship to withstand the brokenness and sinfulness of the people. In the conversation above, Dan notes the importance of the sacrament of reconciliation (or confession) in the Catholic tradition, which ritualizes forgiveness. In and through the sacrament, we celebrate God's gracious mercy.[19] In essence, we accept God's invitation to renew the covenant, con-vert our hearts, and enter more deeply into relationship. God's refusal to hold grudges or allow sinfulness to have the final word calls us to the same in marriage.

In *Becoming Friends*, Paul Wadell admits that "forgiveness may sometimes seem a preposterously unreasonable love to practice, but the Gospels make it clear that such unreasonable love does not begin with us but with God. [Recall Kasper's argument that mercy is the essence of God.] No one loves more unreasonably than God does. No one loves with more reckless abandon than God does. We may be extravagant lovers, but we are no match for a God who refuses to allow millennia of waywardness to dampen his love."[20] Wadell notes therefore that when Christians forgive, it is "only our feeble attempt" to imitate "the divine madness of a God who finds it much more life-giving to forgive than to condemn."[21]

Laura Rader reflects this understanding when saying, "I think forgive-ness is divine. I don't know that we can forgive others unless we really have God's help or God's grace with that because I think that's a really hard thing to do. But we *do* forgive each other." One man acknowledged that "pride might get in the way" when trying to resolve conflict, "which is why forgiveness is important. I know I need that a lot." He added that it is especially difficult to ask for, or offer, forgiveness when "you feel wounded about something."

Many couples noted that prayer helps. As Dan reminded his focus group, when reciting the Our Father, Christians pray for the grace to forgive those who trespass against us, just as God has forgiven us.[22] Perhaps we can think of moments in our own experience when, following prayer, we have been surprised by a softened heart that allowed us to forgive someone we love with "reckless abandon."

Some couples make it a priority to verbally ask for forgiveness, to apologize when they are wrong. Jim and Anne Marie Donlan, who made dinner at the family table a daily ritual at their house, also talked about ritualizing apologies and acknowledgments of forgiveness for their children. Anne Marie reflected on the fighting that took place in their home ("I mean, no family is perfect."). She told us that whenever she yelled at one of their kids in anger, she would later say to them, "'I didn't handle that very well. You're still in trouble, but I'm sorry for the way I reacted. That probably could have been changed a bit.'" Jim said, "You have to have stuff that you can count on. And even through the struggles and the stuff that you fight about, our kids could count on the fact that we would apologize. I was never afraid to go and say, 'I'm sorry.'" Anne Marie added, "If we thought that we were wrong." "Yeah," Jim agreed. "Not 'You're off the hook and you're not in trouble anymore,' but 'I'm sorry for the way it went.' They could even count on that. They could probably even count on it getting ugly for a while before the apology!" [Laughter].

Even though Jim and Anne Marie may have been responding in anger to a real injustice—to something unkind, disrespectful, or disobedient that their children did—they were nevertheless willing to apologize for their own less-than-generous or inappropriate behavior in response. Anne Marie told us that their children learned from the behavior that was modeled for them. They "would come back if they had a bad moment" and tell her, "Mom, I'm sorry that I said that to you."

The Donlans habitually apologize quite readily, but this is not so in every household. We learned that while some spouses are quick to apologize and forgive, others (like Beth Johnson above) find it difficult to say "I'm sorry," and some are slower to let go of anger and grudges. Nancy Brady reflected on the differences in the way that she and her husband, John, deal with conflict: "John is very forgiving and just okay, it's done, it's over with," whereas "I am a stewer. So he'll kind of put a feeler out in terms of interacting with me just to see: is she done stewing? Does she need more time? And I am better, I don't spend as much time stewing as I used to." Self-critically, Nancy said:

> I don't take any power in the fact that I do that. Some people could really look at it like, 'I'm going to make him pay.' I don't really like that about myself, that I can't let things go, so I don't use that as a weapon, use it as a chance to make him feel bad. I just stay within myself and stay quiet in order to get over it. For me, that is important that I don't take advantage of his good nature. Because we are so different, it could have caused a lot of problems where we really wouldn't be together today because of it. And I am not patting myself on the back. I am not proud of the fact that I can just be like *arrrrrgh* for hours and hours.

Nancy thoughtfully tries not to let her need to retreat and be quiet be used as a passive aggressive "weapon" or a way to lord power over John. She actively tries to avoid "tak[ing] advantage of his good nature" and works to change what she sees as a negative habit of holding onto anger for long periods of time. Nancy sees this tendency as an "imperfection" and strives to be more like her husband. She says, "Because I have him in my life I can work through this. And I don't hold on to things as long as I used to when we first got married, maybe by the time I close my eyes I'll be more like him. . . . Because of the marriage, I have hope that things will get better."

Despite their differences, John and Nancy work hard to resolve conflict and reconcile whenever they have offended the other. John comments, "It's not about selfishness. If I'm hurting her, then what can I do about it? I've got to fix it. And we both have that attitude."

So how do couples know that the problem has been fixed or that they have been forgiven? As noted above, some spouses regularly verbalize apologies ("I am sorry for. . .") and acceptance of those apologies ("I forgive you."). Others express forgiveness by offering a rub on the back, a hug, or a kiss, or simply by stepping back into the marital or family routine after some distance to "cool off." Jerry Simms said, "I know that if I can get a hug or kiss out of it, everything is fine because, if it's not fine, that [gesture] probably wouldn't be offered. But we do make a point, especially if the kids know that we've been disagreeing on something, of being affectionate in front of them, too, so they know that everything's okay." "Yeah, that's true," agreed Lisa. Jerry admitted, "Maybe sometimes a little over the top. [Laughter.] We'll dance in the kitchen. Sing a duet. And then they'll be like, 'Oh God! Oh, I didn't need to see that!'"

Still, spouses are perceptive enough to know when an apology—or offer of forgiveness, for that matter—is insincere—based on tone of voice, body language, or subsequent behavior. One man rightly pointed out that apologies are empty when the same inappropriate behavior continues following it. "For me. . . if the [person is] truly sorry, is there a [corresponding] change of behavior over time? I can see, 'Oh, you *were* sorry because you tried to change that, knowing that it hurt me. So there are words, but there's also action."

We might liken this to the sacrament of reconciliation. Clearly, participation in the sacrament is not meant to be a process that simply offers a clean slate so that one can leave the confessional and continue the same sinful behavior. The Act of Contrition recited during confession includes an acknowledgment of sin, a request for God's forgiveness, *and* a firm commitment to make amends and avoid sin in the future. "I am sorry with all my heart" is followed by "I firmly intend, with the help of your Son, to make up for my sins and to love as I should."

And so it goes in marriage—changed behavior concretizes an apology and proves its sincerity. The sacrament of reconciliation, as well as the ritual of asking for and receiving forgiveness in marriage (and family), is meant to foster growth of persons as well as renew and deepen relationship.

The Way of Fidelity: You Make a Marriage Work

It is work. You make a marriage work to keep it strong. . . . You have to want to make it work, and you have to put in time as well as you have to negotiate; it's a give and take. Between living with somebody, being married to them, then the complications of bringing children into the world, everybody has to change their ways and work at it. [Since] both of us [had] a strong family and faith base growing up, it's just sort of natural that that's what you do. You're not always going to get along, but in the end you do whatever you need to do to make it work.

Mike Vandenbusch is one of many who described fidelity as a "natural" expectation for themselves based on faith commitments and family experience—"that's what you do." Yet the emphasis within Mike's description of permanent commitment is on the *effort* and *work* of both partners in marriage. He confirms Lawler's argument that indissolubility is an ongoing task that spouses undertake. Defending and sustaining the marital relationship over time takes work. Entering into the chaos of one's flawed partner in order to meet his or her needs "until death" takes work. Sharing life in married partnership, with its inevitable conflict and suffering, takes work. Parenting, with all of its "complications," takes work. In light of this, we reiterate and affirm the claim made by one man in our study: "Marriage is not for punks." Punks are immature and unreliable, and therefore not up to the demands of authentic commitment.

In her text that explores the vices in modern life, Rebecca Konyndyk DeYoung warns that the traditional deadly sin of "sloth" is a threat against marital fidelity: "The slothful person, in this sense, is one who resists the effort of doing day after day after day whatever it takes to keep the bonds of love strong and living and healthy, whether he or she feels particularly inspired about doing it or not."[23] She writes:

> Sometimes marriage and other friendships feel euphoric and energizing; other times, they are tedious, empty, wearying routines, or just plain work. The point is that being committed to any love relationship takes daily nurturing, daily effort, and daily practices that build it up. Neglecting these will slowly break the relationship down. Nurturing grudges or selfish claims instead will erode it and make us resentful of a relationship that now feels like a suffocating trap . . . It is through daily practices and disciplines, whether we feel like doing them or not, that the decision to love is renewed and refreshed, and the commitment of love is kept alive.[24]

Recall that when couples exchange vows and rings they yield a claim to the one they love and are subsequently bound in future choices to be faithful to that claim, or to betray it. Theologian Margaret Farley explains that when we make a commitment to love and be faithful in our marriage vows, we are effectively committing ourselves to "do the deeds of love" in the future.[25] One promises to be willing to *do* what is best for the other in the future: care for the other, meet the needs of the other, serve the other—in essence do "all that one can" to affirm and support the other's life and well-being.[26] The sin of sloth tempts one to refuse to live up to that promise by being unwilling *today* to do the deeds of love, unwilling to meet the demands of one's covenantal promise.

Farley argues that there is a "way of fidelity," a way of thinking, being, and acting that fights against sloth and honors the freedom that we have to make daily choices about our love. Farley maintains that three kinds of experiences constitute potential crises for fidelity to committed love: (1) conflicting desires, (2) loss of original vision, and (3) loss of presence.[27]

First, practicing the way of fidelity means that one does not give in to *conflicting desires*, such as the desire to free oneself from marital or family commitments (to simply walk out when facing challenges) or the desire to enter into a romantic relationship with someone other than one's spouse. Farley suggests that when conflicting desires (that threaten fidelity) arise, one must actively "renounce" them and reaffirm one's commitment. In her words, fidelity requires that there not only are certain ways that I cannot act, but "there are certain ways I cannot allow myself to *think*."[28]

This way of fidelity is reflected in the testimony of spouses who say "divorce is not an option," as many stated in our interviews. Divorce is not on the table for discussion. It is not thrown out as a threat during arguments. It is not imagined or considered as a possibility. Thus, couples do not even *think* about it. Sarah Ruffalo said, "It cannot ever be an option. And if it's not, then you are going to work [at] making it better, making it through—just, I couldn't imagine waking up everyday and wondering, do I really want to be married to you or not? I can't! He's my husband, my kids' father. His siblings are my in-laws—it just is, it's done."

Lisa and Jerry Simms lamented the fact that some of their friends have divorced due to infidelity. In reflecting upon this, Lisa talked about the wedding day being "just the beginning" of a lifetime commitment that is not primarily about romance. "It's ongoing, and you need to evolve and you need to grow together." Jerry notes that "the newness and the excitement, the romance [of the early relationship] is still there, but it's not the overarching thing that's [keeping] you together."

Lisa believes this is important for young people to know, and she talks to her younger coworkers about it, because they seem to have overly romantic ideas about marriage. "[W]hen my friends' marriages have broken up because of infidelity, I think that is why—they got so excited to meet somebody new, or to talk to somebody online . . . to a few people it's happened that way . . . they get into a chat room and get talking to somebody who makes [them] feel so special and exciting . . . they get that excited feeling again and then it all falls apart."

"It falls apart" because the person has failed to renounce a conflicting desire. If Lisa's assessment is correct, in these cases the desire to feel romantic attention and excitement led to choices of betrayal rather than fidelity. Farley suggests that, if facing conflicting desires, "I should 'stop' long enough to hear the voice within me that is most truly mine. If, halting there, I understand that I do not want to betray what I have chosen to love, then I cannot (even in my imagination) play games that will threaten that bond. I must not begin what will lead where I do not ultimately want to go."[29] For this reason, setting careful boundaries is crucial.

The reality that Lisa and Jerry Simms describe—the lessening of romantic feelings—can be the result of what Margaret Farley calls a "loss of original vision." It is a loss, she argues, that can threaten fidelity. When couples first fall in love, they tend to idealize one another, seeing all the things that are good and beautiful in the other.[30] "'Romantic' love . . . is love that rises from our whole self in response to an 'original vision' of the beloved as beautiful, as wholly loveable."[31] But this vision cannot last. In fact, "there is an inevitability to its fading" as a spouse gets to know his or her partner more intimately, and his or her imperfections and weaknesses are revealed more fully over time.[32]

Inevitable as it is, in Farley's words, "Everything depends on how we interpret the loss of vision." She notes that, following a loss of original vision, we may believe that we see our spouse *more clearly* than we did before, that we now know what he or she is *really* like, and what we see is far from ideal. But there is also the possibility "that we actually see *less well* than we did originally, that what we have come to know is less centrally characteristic" of our partner than what we first saw.[33] In the latter case, "what we first saw [the goodness and beauty of our early idealization] is real, and remains real. The problem is with our seeing, not with the beauty of the beloved."[34]

Therefore Farley suggests: "The way to keep love alive is to try to keep seeing, and our only hope of continuing to see is to keep looking. Even believing involves keeping watch, keeping vigil, seeing through memory and through hope. And when we do see directly, we can come to see better as we 'attend' more carefully, more consistently—as we heighten our capacity to see."[35] We have a choice: we can look generously and lovingly on our spouse—actively trying to see what is beautiful (believing that what we saw in our original vision is still present), or we can see in a "pinched" way, concentrating on all of the negative qualities of our spouse, all of the ways that he or she fails to meet our expectations, that builds resentment.[36]

Above, Beth Johnson spoke about her willingness to simply "overlook" her husband's faults "because she loves [him]." She refuses to let the things that annoy her about Joe dominate her vision, and she appreciates that he does the same for her. Gretchen Baker actively tries to build up her spouse's "true talents and virtues" by praising and encouraging them rather than "concentrating too much on the weak points" that she chooses to "forgive." Gretchen recognizes the power of *choosing* to see and celebrate what is good in her partner rather than holding onto and making central his weaker points. In doing so, she practices fidelity.

Farley highlights the role that memory and hope plays in nourishing our commitments. She explains that remembering is our way "to hold the past in the richness of the present, hoping is our way of both embracing and expanding the horizons of the future." To illustrate this idea, Farley offers the example of the prophets of Israel, who "called the people to remember their past—the promises made to them and their response" and thereby "called them to remember 'who you are.' In this remembering, the people could be thrust toward a future: the future that is promised."[37]

Remembering the establishment of the covenantal relationship with God reminded the people of their current identity as *people of God* and gave them hope for a future enriched by the promises of God. Anniversaries offer an opportunity for spouses to remember why they fell in love with their spouse (original vision) and to recall the beauty of their early relationship and the joy of their wedding day. Remembering the fullness of love and promise that existed in turn brings that love and promise into the present (spouses remember "who we are") and gives hope for the continued fulfillment of those promises in the future.

Of course, memory does not only function in this way on anniversaries. Psychologist Judith Wallerstein explains that weaving happy memories and early idealizations of one's partner "into the fabric of daily life" gives the relationship "a meaning that lifts it above the mundane."[38] Memory "helps to mute the inevitable disappointments that occur in every relationship. The powerful memories provide a reservoir of past indulgences on which people can draw when things look dark" or when things seem dull.[39] Sarah Ruffalo described an interesting method she uses for remembering what is good about her spouse:

> I'm a big score-keeper. And in our first year of marriage, I kept score on everything. I would get angry and resentful toward him because I was always doing more and doing it better. And some-thing—I think I read a book . . . was about keeping a journal of all the happy things that happened, and it kind of hit home for me. Why am I writing down all the stuff that makes me mad? And so I have something called "The Brendan Book" and I write down all the things that make me happy. If I feel joy, I try to write it down at the end of the day. So when I am feeling irritated or mad at him, I read that. It has been a nice tool for me personally; it softens—I'm keeping the good score now instead of the bad score. It helps a lot.

When Sarah is "irritated or mad" at Brendan, happy and joyful memories "soften" her irritation and make her grateful for Brendan's good qualities. "The Brendan Book" functions as "her reservoir of past indulgences" on which she draws.

Weaving memory into daily life also uplifts and brings deeper meaning to the marriage of Al and Christine Kozak. Christine acknowledges that when "people are married so long and they know each other so well," there is a temptation to focus on the negative. Therefore, she offers this advice: "Don't focus on those negative little things because there are so many other wonderful, good things to focus on. Those are the qualities, think about why you fell in love with that person, why you love that person, think back to while you were dating and, you know, it could just be looking at old pictures, or watching old movies together, just thinking back . . . reliving how we used to look in our twenties even! All the nostalgia . . ." Yes, all of the nostalgia, and in particular periodically revisiting treasured memories with one's spouse, has a way of enriching the present.

In addition, the Kozaks shared a story that vividly illustrates the power of memory in sustaining commitment and enriching the present. Each year, Al and their five children make a special meal for Christine, as "a thanks for Mom for doing all the hard stuff she does." The children and Al do the menu planning, shopping, cooking, and decorating, usually around a special theme—Christine is the guest of honor. Smiling warmly, Christine said, "Those little things stay with me forever. I always think about that and when I am having a bad day or the house is a mess . . . [I think], *but remember that lovely dinner I had two weeks ago? I always have to think back, okay, it doesn't matter that there are Cheerios all over the floor or my daughter spread peanut butter all over her hair because I still had that really nice dinner.*"

Working to see the goodness in our partner and in our relationship—through attentive seeing and memory—helps us fight against what Farley calls "loss of presence." There is a danger in becoming disengaged emotionally over time, so that one merely goes through the motions rather than being fully present and truly connected in the marriage commitment. Granted, there may be times where a kind of constancy is all we can offer—times when we force ourselves to do the deeds of love, but there is no joy in it; we do what is daily necessary to hold up our commitment, but we do not "feel" connected.

But constancy alone is not enough. Farley acknowledges that there *is* a place for constancy in the way of fidelity, that constancy "can . . . even represent the greatness of our love: our decision to stay in relation, to affirm the one we love, to do the deeds of love whether we 'feel' present or not."[40]

Constancy ought to be connected to fidelity, in which one is "present" in the deeds of love and in which one strives to overcome any feelings of emotional absence or staleness in the relationship. Remember James Keenan's point that began this chapter: fidelity is not just not walking out on a commitment, not just remaining in a commitment because one is obligated to do so. Rather, fidelity requires doing all that one can to sustain and defend a commitment. Working to communicate well with one's spouse, especially in the midst of conflict; forgiving one's spouse, again and again; staying emotionally connected to one another insofar as possible; practicing the way of fidelity that renounces conflicting desires, remembers and hopes, and strives to maintain presence and a generous and loving view of one's spouse—these are ways of defending and sustaining relational commitment.

The Gift of Fidelity: A Deep Sense of Joy

"I don't know what is more important in a marriage than fidelity and trust in fidelity," said Phil Rullo. He understands fidelity as "the honesty with which you practice your life on a daily basis, the transparency you show in communication with the other person so that trust may result finally in that kind of fidelity." He told us that, in their fifty-two years of marriage, "there was never a time" when he mistrusted his wife, Jane, or "was concerned about her faithfulness. Never a time. Never even came close. And so when I think of fidelity, I think of that. I think of fidelity, too, as upright support. To be steadfast in the support you offer to someone."

Phil explained that fidelity is crucial because marriage "is fraught with problems and concerns," and so "practic[ing] honesty and good communication" and offering "steadfast support" is necessary. His wife, Jane, agreed with Phil's description of fidelity and added, "When you really care about the other person, then that [fosters] fidelity, because if you know that someone really loves you and they put you first, you are not out looking for anything anywhere else . . . I think there can be nothing better than to know that that other person is putting you before them."

In our interviews with couples, again and again we heard this kind of absolute trust in, and deep gratitude for, the fidelity of their spouses. One husband, who grew up in an abusive home and therefore had a difficult time "letting people in" and trusting people, began to cry when speaking of his wife's "devotion" to him. "I trusted her and I always have. She's never let me down these forty years."

Another woman recalled a time in her forty-eight-year marriage when she was struggling with depression and seeing a therapist: "I was very angry with my husband and [the therapist] said, 'Well, do you think he would ever cheat on you?' And I said, 'Absolutely not.' And she said, 'Well, are you sure?' I said, 'Absolutely not!' That was the most ridiculous thing I've ever heard. And that's what I truly believe. What we had was going to remain even if there were problems, that *we* were going to be there."

Such confidence in the faithfulness of one's spouse is a great gift, and one for which many spouses expressed appreciation.

Indeed, marriage is "fraught with problems," and there are "ebbs and flows" within every married relationship; fidelity offers confidence that the relationship will nevertheless withstand these challenges and seasons. Jeanne Carter said, "One thing that brings me joy . . . is knowing of Mark's fidelity. And on the whole spectrum of emotions, wherever I am, I know that he is faithful, and he has promised me that he will be faithful so that gives me a deep sense of joy even if I am crabby on the outside. But [his fidelity provides] confidence or something like that."

Jeanne mentioned finding comfort in Mark's fidelity in the face of family struggles, insecurities about her body, sickness, and "icky" moods in the house. She said, "We've always come through those icky times and I think that we have confidence that we know we'll get there, to the better times. But the fidelity is the day to day grind."

Sally Mahon said, "Fidelity to both of us is something we treasure a lot. For me, it just seems natural that I would be faithful. But you do have to work at really living that out." She believes that she could be "more faithful in appreciation" of her husband, whose goodness and loyalty she sometimes takes for granted. "He knows I'll always be faithful to him until my last breath. But to be more appreciative . . . you have to be mindful of building each other up and affirming . . . the longer you are together, the more you are proud of that stick-to-it-ive-ness. And I think that's what fidelity is, even when it is not all easy and fun."

Sophia Vandenbusch appreciates the benefits of the fidelity she and Mike have shown throughout their sixteen-year marriage, that has included times far from "easy and fun": a challenging first year of marriage away from their emotional support system; the loss of a child; frequent separation due to Mike's travel for work (that involves emotional hardship but also the difficulty of managing care for their three children); and the death of Mike's mother, aunt, and beloved sister within a short period of time. Sophia said:

You do reap the rewards [of fidelity] because when you're in the bad times, you have a lot of emotion involved—not that you don't with the good times, too, but—all of those negative things, the evil working on you saying 'this isn't worth it, this isn't going to work,' but then when you get through that and you're stronger—we are obviously, without a doubt, much stronger than we were when we got married, when we were in a 'we're in love' kind of a phase. Now we are a strong couple, a strong unit together, probably partly because of the things that we've gotten through and *made the choice to get through*, and not just get through, but get through and become closer and become better.

Sophia's belief that her marriage has "reaped the benefits" of a faithfulness that resulted in a stronger, closer, and better relationship was affirmed by others. In particular, two women made comments to that effect at the conclusion of one of our focus groups, in which we benefited from the accumulated wisdom of 202 years of marriage.[41] One woman said, "Looking back, you think fifty-five, fifty-six years ago, when you first got married, you were so naïve! And all that wisdom and age together you gained and accomplished together, you know?" [Nods of agreement all around.] The other woman added, "I often think of those that don't make it through.[42] Every marriage has a tough time. It's so sad to never see the other side! And you come out stronger and bond so much more when you come through that. And when you don't, it's sad."

Conclusion

Learning from the Saints

Vatican II's *Lumen Gentium* (The Dogmatic Constitution on the Church) reminds Catholics of the universal call to holiness. Each person—lay and ordained alike—shares this vocation to holiness, this call to sainthood. For most adult Catholics, it is within the context of vowed, married life that the joyful and challenging path to sainthood is traveled. Yet it is well known that the bulk of canonized saints are single rather than married. Further, the stories of married saints often seem sanitized from the sweat, blood, and passion of married life—for example, by emphasizing the "holy" part of a saint's life that followed the death of a spouse (e.g., Elizabeth Ann Seton) or praising the willingness of a couple to live chastely as brother and sister after raising children (e.g., Luigi and Maria Betrame Quattrocchi). This is a reflection of the historical emphasis in the Catholic tradition of the superiority of the celibate, consecrated religious life to the married life as a path to holiness.

Tellingly, a few people in our study told us that, at the time of their marriage, they considered the married life as a kind of "second best" option—that is, not quite as holy as becoming a priest or a nun, but still right for them. Those who seriously considered entering the vowed religious life indicated that they felt significant guilt about choosing a "lesser" path in the vowed, married life. One man stated that his decision to marry rather than become a monk was considered quite a disappointment to his parents, and—for years—they did not seem to tire of reminding him so!

Of course, we are in a different moment in the church, and contemporary magisterial teaching more readily acknowledges the goodness of the vocation of marriage and family. Nevertheless, we still have work to do within the church to help married people recognize the holiness in their ordinary lives and to honor the everyday, married saints among us. This text is one small contribution to that effort insofar as it celebrates the holiness within the sometimes messy, complicated lives of "married, everyday saints" and sees those lives as fertile ground for theological thinking about marriage and, more broadly, about Christian discipleship.

We hope by now it is clear that while we see the married couples in our study as "everyday saints," as models of holiness, they are not perfect people, nor are their marriages without struggle and difficulty. We recall one couple that told us that the day before their interview they had been furious with one another—they were arguing and spent much of the day in frustrated silence. Not surprisingly, they wondered just how they were going to come the next day to talk to us about their happy marriage as a model of holiness! But the partners reconciled, and they came, and we were grateful for their wisdom. They told us beautiful stories about the goodness of their relationship and their family life. They told us, honestly, about their daily efforts—and their reliance on grace—to live out the gospel together. In that way, though imperfect like the rest of us, they were perfect for our project.

Indeed, our contention is that marriage is a *workshop* for everyday saints—it is a context where two gather to learn and practice the methods and skills needed for flourishing relationship and holiness. It is a context in which two imperfect people strive to ever-deepen communion with one another and God. The work is ongoing because discipleship is ongoing, and conversion is a lifetime's task.

We cannot adequately express our gratitude for the fifty couples—masters in the workshop—who agreed to be interviewed and to teach us about the methods and skills they have honed together. We were astonished by their willingness to trust us with their stories, despite the vulnerability that accompanies talking about personal experiences and the most precious relationships of their lives. Truly, it was our joy and privilege to hear from these people—so honestly and so openly—about how faith impacts their married relationship and how their married relationship impacts their faith. We were moved by their stories: laughing—often, and occasionally hysterically—and sometimes crying—out of sympathy, or admiration, or both. We were moved by the goodness revealed to us in their lives, at least some of which we hope we have revealed to you in the pages of this text. These couples entrusted a tremendous gift to us by sharing their stories, and we feel a great responsibility to pass along their wisdom, so that others can learn from them. We hope we have done them justice.

A Final Word to Married Couples

Simply, we ask you to embrace, celebrate, and nurture the holiness of your married lives. Envisioning your own marriage as a workshop for holiness, we hope that the stories of these married couples inspire you to:

1. Deepen the friendship that you share with your spouse. And, together, deepen the friendship you have with God.

The couples in our study emphasized the importance of authentic friendship in marriage. As Christian married friends, they model virtue for one another; act unselfishly and teach one another to care; support and challenge one another; live out their faith commitments together, guided by the Christian narrative; and, lest we forget, enjoy one another's company! Ultimately, these married friends are committed to, and work for, one another's flourishing and holiness—friendship with God is the end that drives their daily choices and behaviors.

We hope these couples inspire you to work tirelessly for the good of your partner, in whom you delight. Honor and foster the intimacy that you share. Give thanks for it. Practice patience and a generous attentiveness so that daily struggles and challenges, human limitations and weaknesses, do not cause you to lose sight of the goodness and beauty in your married and family life.

In addition to paying attention and lifting up what is good, use memory to inspire appreciation and gratitude. Celebrate one another, support one another, and—when necessary—challenge one another. Remember that you have chosen to practice your discipleship in partnership, and your central goal is to help one another flourish in communion with the Living God.

2. Love one another passionately and justly.

The couples in our study respect the power of their sexuality, seeing it as a good gift from God, designed to bring them into loving communion. They celebrate and nurture that gift, expressing it thoughtfully and well, not only in the bedroom, but in every room. They find ways to "stay connected" with one another, knowing that mutual affection and a vibrant sexual relationship is one important part of a flourishing marriage. They honor the fact that sex is not simply recreational but creates real connections and consequences, and they take responsibility for their sexual behaviors.

We hope that these couples inspire you to nourish your sexual relationship with your partner, who is your beloved and your equal. Strive for fidelity, justice, and mutuality in your relationship broadly and in your sexual relationship specifically. Remember that the erotic love at the heart of marriage is not only meant for your good as married partners, but for the good of family and the wider world, as illustrated in the lives of the couples we interviewed. Let your love flow outward and be life-giving, "bringing more God into the world."

3. See your marriage as a fruitful place to encounter God.

The couples in our study clearly show that God is not only encountered at church on Sundays, or during intentional prayer, but also at the family table; in the treasured rituals unique to each home; in daily care for one another's body and spirit; and in shared sorrow and delight. The sacramental worldview is nurtured in the sacramental life of the church, but participation in that life ought to train our eyes to see holiness in everyday life and in one another, in the ordinary activities of our daily lives.

We hope you will follow the example of these couples. Sustain the rituals that mark and celebrate the presence of God in your midst. Open your eyes. Be astonished. Give thanks. Share the joy.

4. Practice mercy.

The couples in our study find ways to be hospitable and serve one another in their homes, and also to practice mercy outside of their homes. Through various stages of married life (e.g., raising small children, juggling dual-careers, managing active family schedules, caring for aging parents), they creatively support one another's efforts to extend mercy in the wider community and to balance those efforts with responsibilities within the home.

We hope their stories inspire you to find ways to expand the love that you share in your marriage and family to include others. Intentionally and continually widen your circle of love. Open your doors to those in need, offering a hospitable welcome. Further, take the risk to wander outside your home in order to actively seek out the neighbor in need, the one who is not likely to knock on your door, but who nevertheless needs to be fed, given drink, visited, comforted, loved. In light of *your* circumstances and responsibilities, commit to be partners in practicing mercy.

5. Support one another in suffering.

We knew prior to embarking on this project that no person, no couple, no family escapes suffering in this world. But the couples in our study powerfully show us that holiness *can* be expressed and deepened in the midst of suffering, tragedy, and grief. Rather than seeking comfort in easy theological answers that justify suffering or turn it into a good, in painful times these couples courageously maintained faith in a God who loves them and remains present with them, and hope in a God who does not allow suffering to have the final word.

Beyond anchoring themselves in trust and hope in God, these couples *made present* God's love in and through the understanding and care they exhibited for each other, even as they engaged suffering in different ways. Many couples describe their emergence from difficult—even seemingly unbearable—moments in their married life surprisingly "closer" and "stronger" because they tenaciously leaned on and supported one another. Further, support from wider communities—in particular prayerful communities of faith—seemed to lighten even the heaviest of burdens.

We hope that you will take heart from the experience of these couples: while you cannot escape suffering, it need not separate you from one another or from God. In light of the testimony we heard, we cannot offer simple solutions, of course. We can only note what has helped these couples endure suffering in their lives: praying—alone, together, and in community; trusting deeply in the goodness of God who is known in the paschal mystery of death and resurrection; being patient with and supporting one another; and leaning on a wider circle of family and friends.

6. Be faithful.

The couples in our study illustrate that fidelity creates the conditions for deep and authentic intimacy, sexual and otherwise. Their experience shows us that faithfulness in marriage is a tremendous *gift* that builds trust and offers freedom and confidence for both partners. Yet it requires work and determination. In this way, fidelity is a *task* that demands that spouses practice a way of fidelity. Indissolubility in marriage is created daily by married partners who *choose* to be faithful to marital vows—in good times and bad, until death do us part—time and time again.

We hope these couples inspire you to practice fidelity, mutually. Take your vows with the utmost seriousness. Be willing to do the deeds of love, even in moments when amorous feelings are absent. Generously offer and accept forgiveness in your relationship. Be faithful sexually, yes, but also be faithful in appreciation. Build one another up. Keep your eyes open to all that is beautiful and good in the one you love.

7. Root yourselves in a community of faith.

As you seek to help one another grow in holiness, rooting your married-friendship-of-two in a wider community of the friends of God provides much-needed support. The couples in our study emphasized time and again (and again) the value of active participation in a church community as they pursue the Christian married life together. Couples described the regular celebration of Mass as a kind of daily or weekly "compass-setting," as a "reset button" that reminds them of what is most important, and as a joyful gathering of church "family" that provides modeling and support as they try to practice the Christian way of life.

Regular participation in a Catholic church community adjusts the moral compasses of the gathered people through the Word and the Eucharist. At Mass, we are shaped by the Scriptures that remind us of the virtues and values that ought to mark Christian married and family life—such as love, generosity, self-sacrifice, justice, mercy, hospitality, service, and fidelity. Ideally, the Scriptures convert us—we take them on, so to speak, and they change our minds and hearts. The Christian narrative can help us to live more hopefully in a culture in which we are exposed to narratives of despair. Moreover, gathering together at the eucharistic table prompts us to remember that we are called to *become* the body of Christ—blessed, broken, and given to others. As we enact Jesus' radically inclusive table fellowship at the eucharistic table, we remember the call to practice hospitality in our own homes and to find ways to show mercy to others when we leave the church building.

At Mass, then, the Scriptures form us in virtue, and the Eucharist provides food for the (often challenging) journey of discipleship; we are thereby strengthened to live out our vocation as married Christians. Our hearts, minds, and spirits are renewed and "reset" so that we might more capably "go in peace to love and serve the Lord."

Finally, connection to a parish family can provide ongoing support and inspiration as you live out your vocation to marriage. In this text, you read about couples being "held up" and "fed" by their parish community during times of difficulty and suffering; couples being inspired by merciful parish leaders and by the service and hospitality of fellow parishioners; and couples being encouraged in their marital and familial relationships by other couples who model steadfast fidelity to one another, year after year. Participation in a parish community thereby strengthens married partners because of the support of the gathered people, who are likewise striving to live and love like Jesus Christ. For all of these reasons, we encourage you to root yourself in a eucharistic community.

A Final Word to Church and Parish Leaders

We hope you will celebrate the goodness of the everyday, married saints that populate the pews, and seek out their wisdom. In addition to a stance in which the magisterium *teaches* about holiness—as it rightly should—the magisterium would do well to also be willing to assume a stance in which it *listens and learns* from the sense of the married faithful about holiness.[1] The church gathered is a pilgrim church—imperfectly living out the gospel and moving toward God—and the saints among us who can teach us about holiness are both celibate and married.

We hope that the church will listen to the experience of holy, married persons about what they can offer the church and what they need from the church; help couples to name, celebrate, and nurture the holiness that permeates ordinary married life; and support couples in their vocation to married and family life. In our interviews, we asked couples to reflect on whether and how the wider church supports their marriages. Here is some of what we learned.

When we asked couples to identify helpful messages or teachings about marriage they have *heard* from church leaders (e.g., in a homily or in a marriage preparation program) or *read* (e.g. in church documents or pastoral letters), they were usually slow to answer. In fact, it was not unusual for couples who otherwise responded easily and profusely to our questions to be brought to silence by this particular question. While one couple mentioned how helpful they find Pope John Paul II's Theology of the Body, *no couple* named a specific church document about marriage and/or family as particularly helpful or influential in an interview or focus group. Keep in mind that the fifty couples with whom we spoke are very active in their parishes; they are folks who are steeped in the Catholic Church. Yet there was little indication that these couples are regularly turning to magisterial documents on marriage and family for guidance.

In fact, when asked this question, a good number of people commented negatively about the magisterium's emphasis on sexual issues, which were the only "official" teachings about marriage with which some couples seemed familiar, except perhaps for the church's teaching against divorce. Others spoke critically (and emotionally) about the enforcement of official restrictions regarding who may receive communion—for example, at interfaith weddings or church gatherings that include non-Catholics. What struck us about these responses was that we asked the couples which teachings or messages from the church they find *helpful*; they talked, however, about teachings that they interpret as largely negative or exclusionary.[2]

But what most surprised us (and moved us) when we asked this question was the number of people who paused and then began talking *about other couples* in their parishes that they see as models of marriage. For instance, one man said, "For me, the church has come to be the people, friends, community. That speaks to me about marriage more than doctrines." Another woman said, "You sit in church and you see the love and the affection. That's one of the things I love. You know, the young couples, the middle-aged couples, the old couples—everybody in between. You can sit in church and you can see the love, the admiration, the respect, the affection that these people still have for each other. You see a husband and wife look at each other and smile or something. It's—we minister to each other in our marriages and I think our marriage is stronger because of what surrounds us."

We find these responses compelling. When directly asked what helpful messages they have learned from the church about marriage, the vast majority of couples did not reference any "official" teaching, document, or lesson from preaching. Instead, they described the presence and influence of married people in the church community who model for them loving and faithful marriage. They talked about the ways that everyday, married people in parishes minister to one another. How sacramental! The "church" message about marriage that speaks most powerfully to them is the message of holiness spoken in the lives of the married couples in their community.

In light of this testimony, we argue that church leaders would do well to consider that even the most active members of the church are not best reached through documents on paper but through the experiences of their lives. What the magisterium desires to teach ought to be grounded in, and enriching for, that experience. And since couples are influenced by models of married-holiness in their communities, church leaders should be intentional about creating and supporting opportunities for couples to engage one another and know one another's stories beyond quick coffee and donut exchanges after Mass.

Based on the testimony of couples in our study, what else did we learn about how the church effectively supports vibrant, Christian marriages? First, many of the couples are actively involved in ministry with engaged couples in their parishes, sharing wisdom with those who are just entering this way of life and assisting in their marriage preparation. In this process, more established couples facilitate conversations with engaged couples, helping them to understand the Catholic perspective on marriage (e.g., its sacramental, covenantal, life-giving nature) and to carefully consider the many aspects of healthy marriages: good communication, healthy sex life, financial cooperation, relationships with extended family, partnership in parenting, and so on. We believe the importance of this ministry cannot be overestimated, especially in a cultural environment that too often overromanticizes marriage, focuses on the wedding day at the expense of the ongoing marriage relationship, and downplays lifelong fidelity and generativity.

A good number of couples also facilitated and/or participated in retreats designed for couples and spoke about the enrichment such organized retreats offer married couples in the Catholic tradition. Donna Erikson said:

> I can remember when we went on a Marriage Encounter and we were married seven years and we dated seven years, and you just think you know him and then it was like, *Whoa! You're opening a new chapter!* Because you thought you knew them and you didn't [fully]. It just keeps getting more and more exciting. And it can! People don't realize that because they are not willing to go out there and help their marriage. They may think that people are going to think their marriage is in trouble. No, these things are to make your marriage better. And if you participate in them, they *will* make your marriage better, and it makes your marriage so much richer than the ordinary. Do you want ordinary? I never want ordinary! Because it doesn't have to be. It can be so much more fun.

Donna Erikson rightly points to the value of ongoing and intentional nurturing and deepening of one's relationship, particularly in light of shared faith. In the same way that one's religious education ought not end when one gets confirmed (often as early as eighth grade), the process of marriage preparation for engaged couples ought not be the end of education about what it means to be married disciples in the Catholic tradition. As Donna points out, couples need not settle for "ordinary" marriages when the extraordinary is possible, and opportunities like retreats for married couples can help them deepen their relationship with one another and God.

Other kinds of programming in parishes—directed at strengthening marriage—serve the same end. For example, we heard of one parish that organized an ongoing program for couples that involved shared reading and discussion about the married relationship along with organized date nights. Ten years later, one man said, "I didn't realize how much of an effect it would have on us, but it's really driven a lot of good things for our marriage."

Explicit marriage ministries were not the only ways that marriage is nurtured in church communities, however. For example, many couples mentioned participation in various small faith communities in their parishes, which strengthened their faith, broadly, and their marriages, specifically. In one focus group, Thomas O'Brien asked:

Did we say how important small faith groups have been to our
parish? [Nods of affirmation all around.] Oh man, they are very
important. We've been in it from the beginning. And at one time
I think they were just for Advent and Lent, meeting once a week.
It started out that way and then a number of groups went on all
year. Some groups come and some groups go. These are people that
meet in their houses. That has been a very important thing for us,
and an important thing for our marriage, and for the example that
we gave to our daughter: that's what you do—you talk about God
and neighbor!

Likewise, several parishes in the study participate in Christ Renews His
Parish (CRHP), which consists of formal retreats with other parishioners,
often followed by regular meals, prayer groups, and Bible studies. Donna
Erikson explains that CRHP provides an opportunity to get to know more
intimately the people in your parish that you may see but not really know
because "you're busy with work and life." She notes, "It's really awesome.
The people you do go on that weekend with, you really feel like you are
sisters and brothers. Now we come together as friends."

Gretchen Baker laughed when telling us that she likes her husband, Jack,
better when he attends his weekly men's prayer group. "He comes home
happier." Jack's morning prayer group grew out of a Cursillo retreat that he
attended in 1999. On the retreat, he learned that there were other men who
wanted to have conversations about faith, conversations beyond superficial
"work talk and everything else." Jack explained that the members of the
group hold each other accountable by focusing on questions such as: Are
you studying? Are you reading? Are you learning? And, most fundamentally: What are you doing to live out your faith? Beyond prayer, the group
provides an opportunity to share "your faith, your struggles, your triumphs
and your failures" with trusted friends.

There were also couples who talked about the importance of opportunities to learn about justice and practice mercy in their church and local
communities. Some participated in programs such as JustFaith through
which they studied Catholic social teaching, together with other couples,
and reflected on what it meant for their family life today. Sheila Pickard
spoke vividly about a parish Advent tradition, common in many congre-
gations, of collecting items for families in need. She described a time years
ago when there was less worry over theft, "And we would have boxes in
church all over and people would get their little slip [naming what] they
were supposed to bring: sugar or flour, whatever. There were boxes where

you could put baking goods, canned goods, whatever. But you could see it and my kids just loved it! You could see a marvelous thing because all of these people were giving and you saw all the results of it; I mean it was actually physically there and it was just an incredible thing."

Others spoke of the importance of serving persons who are poor in their area. One woman, responding to an initial focus group date, explained over the phone, "That's the night the men's prayer group makes a meal for the shelter, so I think you'll have trouble getting participants that night." Many spoke about care extended to those hurting, in their parish or local communities, that was organized by a vibrant church community whose leaders and members understood their faith called them outward.

What became clear to us through our conversations with married couples is that the church enriches marriages not only directly—through marriage preparation, marriage retreats, and parish programs to strengthen the married relationship—but also indirectly, by offering and supporting opportunities for spiritual enrichment as well as service opportunities that allow couples to practice mercy in church and community.

We affirm the many ways that couples are supported in vibrant and committed parishes to live out their vocation to marriage. We implore church leaders at all levels to reflect on how they might best honor, celebrate, and learn from the profound holiness that is embodied in the lives of everyday, married saints.

Appendix

As we designed our research process—benefiting from guidance offered by a sociologist friend who aided us for the price of burgers and beer!—we reminded ourselves often that we are not sociologists. We are not social scientists of any sort. We are a theologian and a minister seeking to ground our work in the richness of lived experience. And we wanted that lived experience to be broader and deeper than our own marriages and those of our closest family and friends. To that end, we developed a research process that would enable us to listen attentively to the experiences of a large group of couples. Through surveys we reached 168 people representing one or both partners in 88 distinct couples, and then—drawing on couples named in the surveys—we interviewed 50 married couples.

The Scope of Our Research

We identified two Catholic dioceses in the Midwest as the loci of our research. One is geographically expansive and includes rural and small town areas as well as a couple of small cities (less populated than the top 100 cities in the United States) and their surrounding suburbs. The other is a major population center and its highly populated suburbs. Within those two dioceses we identified twenty partner parishes.[1] In identifying partner parishes we sought diversity of setting and population, but also needed a willing parish staff member (nearly always a lay minister) who would serve as our connection to couples in that parish. Our debt to those twenty parish staff members is tremendous!

We made contact with couples through two mechanisms. First, in the summer of 2013 we asked the parish staff member to distribute ten surveys (one for each spouse) to five couples who were married at least eight years, were active in their parishes, and whose marriages appeared to be successful and flourishing. The survey respondents remained anonymous to us as researchers. Survey coding did tell us what parish the respondents came from, which was necessary for the interview stage of our research. One question on the survey invited respondents to identify couples in their parish that they see as models of holiness.[2] This pool of names was utilized to invite participation in interviews—either a couple interview (with a single couple and the researchers) or a small focus group, conducted by the researchers, of no more than four couples. The parish staff member extended invitations to be interviewed, with information on how to contact the researchers directly if interested in participating. From October, 2013 through May, 2014, we conducted twenty-four interviews (twelve couple interviews and twelve focus groups,) reaching a combined total of fifty couples.

The Survey

Surveys were distributed on paper, with separate self-addressed stamped envelopes for each spouse.[3] On occasion, an envelope came back containing surveys from both spouses, but for the most part they were returned to us separately. Surveys were available in Spanish and English, and the parish staff member told us how many were needed in each language.[4] In a few cases a parish staff member requested an additional set of surveys, so the total number of surveys distributed ended up being 210 surveys that were sent to 105 couples. One hundred and sixty-eight surveys were returned, which is a response rate of 80 percent.

We received surveys from each parish contacted; the lowest return rate was four surveys, which was the response from two of the twenty parishes. Five of the twenty parishes returned 100 percent of the surveys. We wondered if gender representation among respondents would be equal, and were pleased to receive surveys from eighty-three men and eighty-five women. Seventy-nine of the couples, or three-quarters of those surveyed, returned both surveys. Eighty-eight couples returned at least one survey.[5] Thus, if a couple responded at all, the likelihood that both spouses returned the survey was very high.

Nearly all survey respondents were parents; only two out of the 168 respondents indicated they did not have children. The survey respondents were nearly all Catholic at the time they were married (91.5 percent indicated this was the case). Of those who were not Catholic, 7.3 percent indicated they were members of another Christian tradition.[6] Below we provide some basic demographic information for those who returned our surveys.

Race/Ethnicity of Survey Respondents	Percent of Total Sample
White/Caucasian	88%
Latino/Hispanic	6%
Black/African-American	4%
Asian/Indian Subcontinent	1%
Native Hawaiian/Pacific Islander	0.6%

Educational Level of Survey Respondents	Percent of Total Sample
Less than a high school diploma	3%
High school diploma	7%
Some college education	22%
College degree	40%
Post-college education	28%

Place of Residence of Survey Respondents	Percent of Total Sample
Rural	18%
Small town	13%
Suburban	42%
Urban	27%

Household Income of Survey Respondents	Percent of Total Sample
Less than $20,000	0%
$20,000–$39,999	9%
$40,000–$59,999	8%
$60,000–$79,999	13%
$80,000–$99,999	19%
$100,000–$119,999	16%
$120,000 or more	35%

Comparison Demographics

We acknowledge that our sample varies from the total U.S. Catholic population in ways that bear noting. As a point of reference, we cite data from the *U.S. Religious Landscape Survey*[7] published by the Pew Forum on Religion & Public Life in 2008. While only 6 percent of our survey respondents indicated they were Hispanic/Latino, this group made up 29 percent of the U.S. Catholic population in 2007.[8] Our sample slightly over-represents African-Americans and under-represents Asian-Americans relative to the 2007 Catholic population. Our respondents indicated higher levels of education than the total Catholic population, for example, 40 percent completed college in comparison to 16 percent in the Pew data, and our sample included nearly three times the number of people with post-college education (28 percent of our respondents versus 10 percent in the Pew research).[9] In the Pew study, 19 percent of Catholics indicated an income of $100,000 or more,[10] whereas in our survey sample 51 percent of respondents had this income level.

We are also aware of data indicating higher levels of marital success for more educated and economically well-off groups, regardless of religious affiliation. For example, an October 2013 report from the Bureau of Labor and Statistics that explores marriage and divorce rates among young Baby Boomers (those born from 1957–1964) indicates that the divorce rate among those who never completed high school is nearly double the rate for those who completed a bachelor's degree or beyond.[11] Those who completed high school but did not attend college, as well as those who attended college but did not complete a four-year degree, were nearly twenty percentage points more likely to experience divorce than those who completed at least a bachelor's degree.[12] Educational attainment and socioeconomic status interface in ways too complex to be considered here. But we note as well this income-related finding from the National Center for Health Statistics: "First marriages are more likely to disrupt in communities with higher unemployment, lower median family income, and a higher percent of families below poverty level or receiving public assistance."[13]

Looking at these points of data tells us that we were in conversation (in person and through surveys) with a group of married couples that was less ethnically diverse, better educated, and richer than the total population of Catholics in the United States today. Our subjects, seen by others as having thriving marriages, were also privileged in their educational and socioeconomic status, factors known to impact marital success in the total population. We see the need for continued study of the experiences of married Catholics, and understand those experiences can be influenced by factors such as culture, education, and income. That said, our aim has been to listen deeply to the life stories of the couples we engaged, and ground our theological and ministerial reflections in their wisdom. It is this task we feel confident we have accomplished.

Survey Gleanings

Below we highlight responses to several survey items from which we draw in the text. The full survey included more items than appear here.

Survey Question 4: How important have the following been for the success of your marriage?

	Extremely Important	Somewhat Important	Not Important	Item Skipped
Balancing shared and individual interests	73%	22%	0%	5%
Courage	43%	38%	10%	9%
Equality	61%	32%	5%	3%
Fidelity/faithfulness to spouse	92%	5%	0%	4%
Financial stability	45%	49%	4%	2%
Forgiveness	87%	10%	1%	3%
Good listening skills	82%	16%	1%	2%
Healthy sex life	48%	45%	4%	3%
Hope	67%	28%	1%	4%
Level of education	18%	54%	27%	2%
Participation in a church community	73%	25%	0%	2%
Patience	80%	17%	0%	2%
Physical attraction	23%	63%	11%	2%
Play/recreation	46%	47%	3%	4%
Self-sacrifice	60%	35%	3%	2%
Sense of humor	71%	26%	2%	2%

continued next page

	Extremely Important	Somewhat Important	Not Important	Item Skipped
Service	48%	46%	4%	3%
Shared morals/values	90%	8%	0%	2%
Shared set of core faith beliefs	82%	16%	0%	2%
Strong family network	71%	24%	3%	2%
Strong friendship network	39%	50%	9%	2%

Survey Question 5: How often has sex with your partner been experienced as the following?

	Never	Sometimes	Often	Very Often	Item Skipped
Affirmation	7%	32%	25%	23%	13%
Celebration	7%	38%	26%	21%	8%
Expression of forgiveness	26%	54%	7%	4%	8%
Expression of intimacy	1%	14%	32%	48%	10%
Holy	29%	27%	21%	11%	11%
Obligation	36%	48%	6%	2%	8%
Play	7%	32%	35%	20%	6%
Pleasure	1%	23%	36%	35%	5%
Renewal	11%	32%	27%	18%	12%

Survey Question 6: Marriage research indicates several common sources of conflict experienced by married couples. How often have the following been sources of conflict in your marriage?

	Never	Sometimes	Often	Very Often	Item Skipped
Child-rearing practices	17%	67%	10%	2%	3%

continued next page

	Never	Sometimes	Often	Very Often	Item Skipped
Communication styles	5%	60%	26%	6%	2%
Demands of parenting	15%	65%	13%	2%	4%
Division of household tasks	29%	55%	13%	1%	2%
Extended family	25%	58%	8%	5%	4%
Finances	20%	55%	15%	6%	4%
Sex	36%	50%	8%	2%	3%
Work/home life balance	21%	52%	17%	4%	6%

Survey Question 7: During times of stress and struggle, how important have the following sources of support been for you?

	Extremely Important	Somewhat Important	Not Important	Not Applicable	Item Skipped
Church community	39%	46%	9%	2%	4%
Church leaders/pastors	28%	42%	18%	7%	4%
Counselors	8%	24%	34%	30%	4%
Family	58%	32%	5%	1%	4%
Friends	43%	47%	7%	1%	2%
Prayer	73%	20%	2%	0%	4%
Sacraments (e.g., Mass, reconciliation)	57%	32%	7%	1%	4%

Survey Question 8: What are three essential characteristics (virtues, values, or practices) that have made your marriage successful? [Note that this was an open-ended question. While the exact wording varied, the responses were categorized through a process of content analysis. Thirty-nine distinct themes emerged. Thirteen of the themes were mentioned by over twenty people.]

Rank	Topic	Count
1	Communication/listening/sharing	43
2	Faith/spirituality	37
3	Forgiveness	33
4	Patience	31
5	Love	29
6	Appreciation/shared time	28
7	Shared values/interests	25
7	Trust	25
8	Humor	24
9	Fidelity/commitment	23
9	Honesty	23
10	Church involvement	22
10	Respect	22

The Interviews

As noted above, one survey question invited respondents to indicate one or more names of couples from their parish who are seen as exemplars of holiness in everyday life. From these names we invited interview participants. Those interviewed as a single couple met with us for ninety minutes, while those in focus groups met with us for two hours. We crafted a single interview protocol but used it flexibly depending on the direction of a particular conversation. Typically we covered about four to six questions from our protocol of over twenty items! Nearly always, the comments couples made would touch on many more topics than we directly asked about. Interviews were recorded and transcribed, giving us the deep narrative woven throughout this text.

We do not have the same demographic information on the interviewed couples as we have for those who completed the surveys. What follows is a demographic sketch we compiled based on what our interview participants shared.

Length of Marriage (in Years)	Number of Couples
8–10	1
11–20	9
21–30	16
31–40	10
41–50	8
More than 50	6

Number of children the couple raised, including biological and adopted children. This does not include children couples took in for a time, often extended family members or their children's friends:

Number of Children	Number of Couples
No children	3
1 or 2	17
3 or 4	21
5 or more	9

Current age range of children. Note this count totals more than 50 as many couples were parents of children in two of these ranges:

Current Age of Child/ren (in years)	Number of Couples
0 – 9	8
10 – 19	12
20 – 29	22
30 and older	21

In addition, five individuals shared that they had been divorced prior to marrying their current spouse, and three individuals shared that they had been in religious life/priesthood prior to marrying.

We recognize the particularities of the couples with whom we spoke impact their experience and understanding of marriage. A couple married eight years with young children, a couple married twenty years with no children and a couple married 50+ years with a gaggle of children, grandchildren and great-grandchildren each has distinct perspectives on the experience of marriage. While we make no claim of statistical representativeness relative to the total Catholic population in the United States, we are convinced the couples we met offer a spectrum of experiences and perspectives that greatly benefitted our thinking, and hopefully served you well as reader.

Notes

Preface   pages ix–xiii

1. *Scripting the Saints*, an invited panel at the Catholic Theological Society of America, June 2011, included Lawrence S. Cunningham, Robert Ellsberg, Fr. James Martin, SJ, and Wendy M. Wright.

2. Authors such as Robert Ellsberg in *The Saints' Guide to Happiness* and James Martin, SJ, in *Becoming Who You Are*, encourage Catholics today to recognize the universal call to holiness, to sainthood, and point out the presence of the saints in our midst—those not officially canonized but nevertheless quietly living as models of discipleship.

3. For the interested reader, the book's appendix treats our methodology, sample demographics, and survey responses in greater detail.

4. "In qualitative research one needs to listen for brilliance. You need to suspend your ideas, assumptions, and knowledge and believe that if you listen hard enough the persons you are listening to will tell you something brilliant that they may not have even thought before. Your listening can pull the brilliance out of them. And that is the truth as that person experiences it." K. E. Edwards, "'Putting my man face on:' College men's gender identity development." Lecture, professional development offering for Mission & Student Affairs staff of St. Norbert College, De Pere, WI, March 2013.

Chapter 1   pages 1–22

1. C. S. Lewis, *The Four Loves* (New York: Harcourt Brace, 1960), 34.

2. Ibid., 35.

3. Beth stays home with her children, who range in age from one to fourteen years old. She and Joe have been married fifteen years.

4. The creation account that appears first in Scripture, Gen 1–2:3 (the priestly account) was actually written later than the story that appears second, Gen 2:4–2:25.

5. Rather than being a proper name, Adam, the word *adam* translates from the Hebrew to mean human being.

6. Paul Wadell, *Becoming Friends: Worship, Justice, and the Practice of Christian Friendship* (Grand Rapids, MI: Brazos, 2002), 77.

7. Ibid, 77. While the Trinitarian God is most typically imaged as Father, Son, and Holy Spirit, this is not the only suitable way to speak about the Trin-

ity. See Elizabeth Johnson's wonderful book, *She Who Is: The Mystery of God in Feminist Theological Discourse* (New York: Crossroad, 1992), for a helpful resource related to naming God.

8. Paul Wadell, *Happiness and the Christian Moral Life* (Lanham, MD: Rowman & Littlefield, 2008), 25.

9. Ibid.

10. Ibid.

11. Wadell, *Becoming Friends*, 72.

12. Ibid.

13. Ibid., 68.

14. Ibid.

15. Richard R. Gaillardetz, *A Daring Promise: A Spirituality of Christian Marriage*, 2nd ed. (Liguori, MO: Liguori/Triumph, 2007), 53.

16. Ibid.

17. Ibid.

18. At times, emphasis on self-sacrifice as an antidote to pride in the Christian tradition has been problematic, especially for women. In 1960, theologian Valerie Saiving wrote an influential essay entitled "The Human Situation: A Feminine View," in which she argues that traditional Christian interpretations of sin as *pride* (that is, an overblown sense of one's own importance) primarily reflect male experience. Saiving argues that, rather than exhibiting pride, women are more prone to "triviality, distractibility and diffuseness; lack of an organizing center of focus; dependence on others for one's self-definition; tolerance at the expense of standards of excellence . . . in short, underdevelopment or negation of the Self." In other words, Saiving argues that women too often lack a strong sense of Self rather than an overblown sense of Self—and *that* is what needs attention. For us, the important implication of Saiving's argument is this: an emphasis on self-sacrifice for those who lack a strong sense of Self—no matter their sex or gender—may be destructive rather than life-giving. See Valerie Saiving, "The Human Situation," in *Womanspirit Rising*, ed. Carol P. Christ and Judith Plaskow (New York: Harper & Row, 1979), 37.

19. Indeed, Jane Rullo attests that Phil has learned to be selfless in their fifty-two years of marriage, appreciating that "he always puts me first, even to the point of a piece of meat—it sounds very minor but if a piece of meat looks a little tougher, he takes that piece of meat and gives me the other. Always making sure that if we go out to eat, 'Where is it that you want to go out to eat?' Not 'I want to go out to eat here.'" Jane notes that these examples may seem minor, but they are indicative of an overall attitude and practice of other-centeredness that permeates their marriage.

20. Margaret Farley, *Personal Commitments: Beginning, Keeping Changing, Revised Edition* (Maryknoll, NY: Orbis, 2013), 136. Historically, of course, the partner with lesser power in patriarchal married relationships is the woman.

21. Herbert Anderson, "Between Rhetoric and Reality: Women and Men as Equal Partners" in *Mutuality Matters: Family, Faith, and Just Love*, ed. Herbert Anderson, Edward Foley, Bonnie Miller-McLemore, and Robert Schreiter (Lanham, MD: Rowman & Littlefield, 2004), 79.

22. Judith Wallerstein and Sandra Blakeslee, *The Good Marriage: How and Why Love Lasts* (New York: Warner, 1995), 239–247.

23. Ibid., 241–242.

24. Ibid., 246.

25. Ibid.

26. Wadell, *Becoming Friends*, 69.

27. Ibid.

28. Ibid., 71.

29. Specifically, 90 percent of our respondents consider shared morals/values to be extremely important; 8 percent think it somewhat important; 82 percent of respondents believe sharing a core set of faith beliefs to be extremely important, while 16 percent think it somewhat important.

30. Oremus is a Catholic prayer study program that encourages personal prayer with Scripture and includes group discussion.

31. Often, encouraging a spouse to attend a retreat, or to regularly meet a prayer group, demands significant sacrifice on his or her part when left to handle childcare and household tasks. Allowing one partner the opportunity for spiritual enrichment of this kind is really a joint venture.

32. "And the scroll of the prophet Isaiah was handed to him. Unrolling it, he found the place where it is written: 'The Spirit of the Lord is on me, because he has anointed me to proclaim good news to the poor. He has sent me to proclaim freedom for the prisoners and recovery of sight for the blind, to set the oppressed free, to proclaim the year of the Lord's favor.' Then he rolled up the scroll, gave it back to the attendant and sat down. The eyes of everyone in the synagogue were fastened on him. He began by saying to them, 'Today this scripture is fulfilled in your hearing'" (Luke 4:17–21).

33. Wadell, *Becoming Friends*, 73.

34. Ibid.

35. Ibid.

36. Pope John Paul II, *Sollicitudo Rei Socialis* (On Social Concern), December 30, 1987, http://www.vatican.va/holy_father/john_paul_ii/encyclicals /documents/hf_jp-ii_enc_30121987_sollicitudo-rei-socialis_en.html.

37. Christians are likely very familiar with one body imagery. We already noted its importance in the creation stories in the Book of Genesis. The New Testament epistles also utilize one body language. See Rom 12, 1 Cor 12.

Chapter 2   pages 23–44

1. Marvin M. Ellison, "Reimagining Good Sex: The Eroticizing of Mutual Respect and Pleasure," in *Sexuality and the Sacred: Sources for Theological Reflection*, 2nd ed., ed. Marvin M. Ellison and Kelly Brown Douglas (Louisville, KY: Westminster John Knox, 2010), 247.

2. C. S. Lewis, *The Four Loves* (New York: Harcourt Brace, 1960), 91. In Lewis's text, *eros* appears as Eros.

3. Sallie McFague, *Models of God* (Philadelphia: Fortress, 1987), 128.

4. Ibid.

5. Rumi, "One Whisper of the Beloved," (Allspirit) http://allspirit.co.uk /one-whisper-of-the-beloved.

6. McFague writes: "The tradition has often turned to the lover model in order to express closeness, concern, and longing between God and human beings; thus, we have the image of God as the faithful husband in Hosea, the Johannine passages in which Christ prays 'that they may be one even as we are one, I in them and thou in me' (17:22b–23a), and of course, the metaphors of the soul as bride to God, in medieval mysticism, or the church as bride of Christ. Some of these images are sexist in subordinating the female to the male, especially the bridal ones, and some are individualistic, especially the mystical ones, but at least they serve as a reminder that the Judeo-Christian tradition [has employed the image of God as Lover]." *Models of God*, 127.

7. Julian of Norwich, *Meditations with Julian of Norwich*, ed. Brendan Doyle (Santa Fe, NM: Bear, 1983), 113.

8. In our written surveys, 48 percent of respondents indicated that a "healthy sex life" is an *extremely important* part of marriage, while 45 percent consider it *somewhat important*.

9. Lewis, *The Four Loves*, 98.

10. See Michael Kimmel's *Guyland: The Perilous World Where Boys Become Men* (New York: Harper, 2008). Kimmel notes how images often present men as sexual aggressors, even violent ones, and women as compliant.

11. Michael Kimmel estimates that gross sales of all pornographic media ranges from $10 to $14 billion annually. Ibid., 170.

12. Catherine Steiner-Adair, *The Big Disconnect: Protecting Childhood and Family Relationships in the Digital Age* (New York: Harper, 2013), 151.

13. Steiner-Adair, *The Big Disconnect*, 183. Kimmel, *Guyland*, 185. Kimmel explains how (traditional) pornography distorts healthy sexuality in part because it reinforces male entitlement to women's bodies. Further, his research shows that young men in particular are often attracted to porn that eroticizes violence and that glamorizes the humiliation of women. He writes: "The world of escape offered by pornography is 'easy.' It makes few relationship demands; it asks little of men morally, intellectually, politically, and offers so much in return: the illusion of power and control." Kimmel, *Guyland*, 179.

151

yland, 189.

ngining Good Sex, 248.

...ely, many young people see hooking up as "the new pathway ...elationships" and—like it or not—the only game in town. Kimmel, ...nd, 214–15.

17. Lewis, *The Four Loves*, 94.

18. Richard R. Gaillardetz, *A Daring Promise: A Spirituality of Christian Marriage*, 2nd ed. (Liguori, MO: Liguori/Triumph, 2007), 78.

19. McFague, *Models of God*, 128.

20. In other words, an openness to children is expected in Catholic marriage. In *Humanae Vitae*, it is stated that couples ought to be open to procreation in "each and every" act of sexual intercourse, unless couples have "serious reasons" for avoiding pregnancy. Paul VI, *Humanae Vitae* (On Human Life), July 26, 1968, http://www.vatican.va/holy_father/paul_vi/encyclicals/documents /hf_p-vi_enc_25071968_humanae-vitae_en.html, sec. 10, 11.

This is not to say that couples must *intend* pregnancy in every act of sexual intercourse, but they are not to block conception with artificial contraception. This teaching, of course, has been hotly debated in the Catholic theological community since the publication of *Humanae Vitae* in 1968. For a helpful discussion of this teaching as well as the critical conversation in the theological community about it, see Richard Gaillardetz's *A Daring Promise*, 81–91. See also Julie Hanlon Rubio, "Beyond the Liberal/Conservative Divide on Contraception: The Wisdom of Practitioners of Natural Family Planning and Artificial Birth Control," *Horizons* 32 (2005):270–94.

21. See *Humanae Vitae*. Or for another discussion of sexual ethics in marriage from a magisterial perspective, see the U.S. Catholic Bishops' document *Marriage: Life and Love in the Divine Plan*, especially the sections entitled "The Two Ends of Purposes of Marriage" and "How Are the Two Ends of Marriage Related?" United States Conference of Catholic Bishops, *Marriage: Life and Love in the Divine Plan* (Washington, DC: United States Conference of Catholic Bishops, 2009), 11–17. http://www.usccb.org/issues-and-action/marriage-and-family /marriage/love-and-life.

22. Highly respected Catholic sexual ethicist Lisa Cahill notes, for example, that while magisterial teaching increasingly stresses women's equality and the value of women's participation in the social and political realm, the tradition must still contend with the deep and troublesome issue "of whether women's advancement requires more flexibility on some of the magisterial sexual norms (especially the ban on contraception) that go back to a time when women were directly and vehemently asserted to be subordinate to men, destined for domesticity alone, and ideally fulfilled as mothers." Lisa Cahill, *Family: A Christian Social Perspective* (Minneapolis: Fortress, 2000), 92.

23. Gaillardetz, *A Daring Promise*, 82.

24. Ibid.

25. Ibid.

26. According to a 2006–2010 National Survey of Family Growth by the Center for Disease Control and Prevention, the number of women ages 15 to 44 with impaired ability to get pregnant or carry a baby to term is 6.7 million. The percent of women ages 15 to 44 with impaired ability to get pregnant or carry a baby to term is 10.9 percent. http://www.cdc.gov/nchs/fastats/infertility.htm.

27. Gaillardetz, *A Daring Promise*, 82.

28. The pressure brought on married couples, especially women, to have children does not come only in church settings, of course. But the church's clear emphasis on procreation can seem a particularly intense pressure.

29. Thankfully, official documents are increasingly recognizing the struggle and pain of infertility. For example, in a pastoral letter, the U.S. Catholic bishops write: "It is true that some marriages will not result in procreation due to infertility, even though the couple is capable of the natural act by which procreation takes place. Indeed, this situation often comes as a surprise and can be a source of deep disappointment, anxiety, and even great suffering for a husband and wife. When such tragedy affects a marriage, a couple may be tempted to think that their union is not complete or truly blessed. This is not true." U.S. Catholic Bishops, *Marriage: Love and Life in the Divine Plan*, 14–15.

30. This sensitivity is important because (a) some married couples who very much desire children are struggling with infertility and (b) persons who are single or who are without children (for whatever reason) should not be made to feel that they are somehow second best or lesser than or not fully living up to their potential as people and as Christians.

31. Cristina L. H. Traina, "Under Pressure: Sexual Discipleship in the Real World," in *Sexuality and the U.S. Catholic Church: Crisis and Renewal*, ed. Lisa Sowle Cahill, John Garvey, and Thomas Frank Kennedy (New York: Crossroad, 2006), 75.

32. U.S. Catholic Bishops, *Marriage: Love and Life in the Divine Plan*, 16.

33. Ibid., 16–17.

34. Brian and Sarah's firstborn son died. They subsequently had two children.

35. "There is now ample evidence that stable and satisfactory marriages are crucial for the well-being of adults. Yet such marriages are even more important for the proper socialization and overall well-being of children. A central purpose of the institution of marriage is to ensure the responsible and long-term involvement of both biological parents in the difficult and time-consuming task of raising the next generation." The National Marriage Project, The State of Our Unions 2011, *When Baby Makes Three: How Parenthood Makes Life Meaningful and How Marriage Makes Parenting Bearable*, ed. W. Bradford Wilcox and Elizabeth Marquardt (Charlottesville, VA: National Marriage Project and the Institute for American Values, 2011), 87, http://www.stateofourunions.org/2011

/SOOU2011.pdf. Furthermore, "In the United States, cohabiting parents are more than twice as likely as married parents to break up." Ibid., 11.

36. In contrast to those who argue that children fare best in two-parent homes that specifically include a mother and a father (as magisterial teaching clearly does), the American Sociological Association states the following: "The social science consensus is both conclusive and clear: children fare just as well when they are raised with same-sex parents. This consensus holds true across a wide range of child outcome indicators and is supported by numerous nationally representative studies." Brief of Amicus Curiae American Sociological Association (ASA) for Respondent Edith Schlain Windsor, *United States v. Edith Schlain Windsor*, Nos. 12–144, 12–307, *31 (February 28, 2013), http:// www.asanet.org/documents/ASA/pdfs/12-144_307_Amicus_%20%28C_%20 Gottlieb%29_ASA_Same-Sex_Marriage.pdf. According to the ASA legal brief, children who are raised since birth by same-sex parents, adoptive parents, and parents utilizing assisted reproductive technologies fare just as well as other children (ASA, 27). Sociological data related to same-sex marriages and parenting by same-sex couples are important to consider when evaluating the morality of these relationships and family structures. We clearly cannot address these matters at any length here. We are drawing on this legal brief because it points to research that shows that marriage can improve child well-being due to the stability it provides, a stability enhanced by social and legal supports.

37. Traina, *Under Pressure*, 75.

38. The obligation for families to extend themselves in mercy and service to the wider community will be examined more fully in chapter 4. A helpful resource for thinking about the responsibilities of Christian families is Lisa Sowle Cahill's *Family: A Christian Social Perspective* (Minneapolis: Fortress, 2000).

39. The National Marriage Project, *When Baby Makes Three*, 47.

40. Ibid.

41. Ibid.

42. See the discussion of a loss of child-centeredness in marriages in the United States in The National Marriage Project's *When Marriage Disappears*, 83 ff.

43. Ibid., 87.

44. Gaillardetz, *A Daring Promise*, 6. He cites *The State of Our Unions Report 2001* by the National Marriage Project.

45. Gaillardetz, *A Daring Promise*, 7.

46. In chapter 6, we will discuss more thoroughly the way of fidelity that maintains Christian marriage over the long haul, a "way" that is much deeper and stronger than fickle and fragile romance.

47. Recall theologian Cristina Traina's words cited above: "children created carelessly by parents who are not committed to a household, who do not see their children as divine gifts, and who do not see the raising of them as a holy task will suffer." Traina, *Under Pressure*, 75.

48. The specific breakdown for how often "division of household tasks" has been a source of conflict in marriage is as follows: 55 percent sometimes; 13 percent often; 1 percent very often. For "work/home life balance" the breakdown is 52 percent sometimes, 17 percent often, and 4 percent very often.

49. The National Marriage Project, *When Baby Makes Three*, 4–5.

50. Ibid.

51. Ibid., 17.

52. We focus on these two factors (*work and family balance* and *sexual satisfaction*) for the following reasons: Regarding *work and family balance*, we think it important to directly address the challenges that couples face trying to balance family obligations and work outside the home, particularly as the number of dual-career couples in our country continues to increase. Further, our feminist commitments prompt us to address the gendered expectations/realities around work and family, especially in light of the Catholic tradition's emphasis on procreation in marriage. Regarding *sexual satisfaction*, since this chapter focuses on erotic love, we thought it appropriate to include some of the report's conclusions regarding the factors that contribute to sexual satisfaction in marriage.

53. The National Marriage Project, *When Baby Makes Three*, 22.

54. Pauline Kleingeld, "Just Love? Marriage and the Question of Justice" in *Mutuality Matters: Family, Faith and Just Love*, ed. Herbert Anderson, Edward Foley, Bonnie Miller-McLemore and Robert Schreiter (Lanham, MD: Rowman & Littlefield, 2004), 24.

55. Ibid.

56. Congregation for the Doctrine of the Faith, *Letter to the Bishops of the Catholic Church on the Collaboration of Men and Women in the Church and in the World*, May 31, 2004, http://www.vatican.va/roman_curia/congregations/cfaith/documents/rc_con_cfaith_doc_20040731_collaboration_en.html, sec. 13.

57. Currently, 47.5 percent of married couples are dual-career. "There are a variety of complex biological, cultural, and personal issues at play, but it's quite common for one partner in a relationship (often the woman) to compromise on his or her career ambitions while the other partner compromises time with family. There is no-one-size-fits-all solution here, but couples need to have open and honest discussions about their ambitions for their careers and their roles in the family, and assure that one partner isn't making all the sacrifice." Jackie Coleman and John Coleman, "How Two Career Couples Stay Happy," *Harvard Business Review Blog*, July 27, 2012, http://blogs.hbr.org/2012/07/how-two-career-couples-stay-ha.

58. Lisa Belkin, "When Mom and Dad Share it All: Adventures in Equal Parenting," *The New York Times Magazine*, June 15, 2008, http://www.nytimes.com/2008/06/15/magazine/15parenting-t.html.

59. Ibid., 3.

60. Ibid., 4.

61. Ibid., 5. Note that housework is defined as things like cooking, cleaning, yard work, and home repairs. Childcare is attending to the bodily needs of children, such as feeding, bathing, and dressing them. Belkin notes that childcare does not "include the fun stuff, like playing and reading and kissing good night." Ibid., 4.

62. Here the report, *When Baby Makes Three*, is drawing specifically on a study on a nationally representative survey of married couples (The Survey of Marital Generosity) that was conducted by Knowledge Networks in 2010 and 2011 and was funded by the Science of Generosity initiative at the University of Notre Dame.

63. Interestingly, Sally Mahon praised the "servant kind of love" that her husband, Pete, shows to her. She is touched when he "anticipates in an amazing way" what might help make things easier for her, even if it is a bit of a sacrifice to him. She offered the example of taking the dog out for a walk, that meant she did not need to do it, "and *that's romantic to me.*"

64. Gaillardetz, *A Daring Promise*, 35.

65. Ibid., 38.

66. Ibid.

67. Anne Marie's parents raised seven children together.

68. Gaillardetz, *A Daring Promise*, 35.

69. The National Marriage Project, *When Baby Makes Three*, 36.

70. Ibid. The report draws upon Janis E. Byrd et al, "Sexuality During Pregnancy and the Year Postpartum," *Journal of Family Practice* 47 (1996): 305–308; and John M. Gottman and Julie Schwartz Gottman, *And Baby Makes Three: The Six-Step Plan for Preserving Marital Intimacy and Rekindling Romance After Baby Arrives* (New York: Three Rivers, 2007).

71. Lewis, *The Four Loves*, 100.

72. Judith Wallerstein and Sandra Blakeslee, *The Good Marriage: How and Why Love Lasts* (New York: Warner, 1995), 192.

73. The National Marriage Project, *When Baby Makes Three*, 36.

Chapter 3   pages 45–64

1. Richard P. McBrien, *Catholicism* (Minneapolis: Winston, 1980), 731.

2. Michael J. Himes, "Finding God in All Things: A Sacramental Worldview and Its Effects" in *Becoming Beholders: Cultivating Sacramental Imagination and Actions in College Classrooms,* ed. Karen E. Eifler and Thomas M. Landy (Collegeville, MN: Liturgical Press, 2014), 13.

3. Susan A. Ross, *Extravagant Affections: A Feminist Sacramental Theology* (New York: Continuum, 1998), 35.

4. United State Conference of Catholic Bishops, *Marriage: Love and Life in the Divine Plan* (Washington, DC: USCCB, 2009), 32.

5. Bernard Cooke, "Christian Marriage: Basic Sacrament," in *Perspectives on Marriage: A Reader*, ed. Kieran Scott and Michael Warren (Oxford: Oxford University Press, 2001), 51.

6. Richard R. Gaillardetz, *A Daring Promise: A Spirituality of Christian Marriage* (Liguori, MO: Liguori/Triumph, 2007), 31.

7. Maureen Gallagher, "Family as Sacrament," in *The Changing Family: Views from Theology and the Social Sciences in Light of the Apostolic Exhortation Familiaris Consortio*, ed. Stanley L. Saxton, Patricia Voydanoff, and Angela Ann Zukowski (Chicago: Loyola University Press, 1984), 10.

8. The importance of family stories shared is explored by Bruce Feiler in *The Secrets of Happy Families: Improve Your Mornings, Rethink Family Dinner, Fight Smarter, Go Out and Play, and Much More* (New York: William Morrow, 2013). Feiler draws on the work of Marshall Duke, a psychologist from Emory University, whose research shows that children who know family stories develop a strong "intergenerational self" and understand that "they belong to something bigger than themselves." Knowing one's family narrative contributes to the resilience of children. In fact, "the more children know about their parents and grandparents, especially their successes and failures, the more they are able to overcome setbacks" (Feiler, 42, 258). Thus, rich family storytelling not only provides occasions of togetherness, and often laughter; it contributes to the well-being of the family members, particularly children.

9. L. Shannon Jung, *Sharing Food: Christian Practices for Enjoyment* (Minneapolis: Fortress, 2006), 30.

10. Ibid., 32.

11. Gaillardetz, *A Daring Promise*, 119.

12. Jung, *Sharing Food*, 135.

13. Ibid., 136.

14. Julie Hanlon Rubio, *A Christian Theology of Marriage and Family* (New York: Paulist Press, 2003), 198.

15. Of all couples surveyed, 93 percent indicated their weddings took place in a Catholic church. Those not married in the church were instructed to skip the items ranking reasons for marrying in the church. Of those married in the church, 81 percent indicated that the desire to have Eucharist as an element in their marriage ceremony was "extremely important" to their decision. The lowest factor was the beauty of the physical church; in fact, nearly one quarter of respondents indicated that the beauty of the church had "no importance" in their decision to marry in a church.

16. USCCB, *Divine Plan*, 33.

17. Ibid., 45.

18. One encounters this language in *Lumen Gentium*, paragraph 11, that concludes: "All the faithful, whatever their condition or state, are called by the Lord, each in his own way, to that perfect holiness whereby the Father Himself is per-

fect." Pope Paul VI, *Lumen Gentium* (Dogmatic Constitution on the Church), Vatican web site, November 21, 1964, http://www.vatican.va/archive/hist_councils/ii_vatican_council/documents/vat-ii_const_19641121_lumen-gentium_en.html.

19. Florence Caffrey Bourg, *Where Two or Three are Gathered: Christian Families as Domestic Churches* (Notre Dame, IN: University of Notre Dame Press, 2004), 25.

20. Ibid., 28–9.

21. Gaillardetz, *A Daring Promise*, 95.

22. Susan A. Ross articulates this on p. 169 of *Extravagant Affections:* "If the sacraments are meant to be mediating signs of grace to the world, transforming the most mundane and the most physical experiences into encounters with God, what better place to ground them than in the life of the family?"

23. Hanlon Rubio, *Christian Theology of Marriage*, 197.

Chapter 4   pages 65–84

1. Jeremy Cotter said this during a focus group conversation about service.

2. Cardinal Kasper defines compassion from a Christian perspective: "One must understand the word *compassion* not only as compassionate behavior. Rather, we must also hear in 'compassion' the word 'passion.' This means discerning the cry for justice as well as making a passionate response to the appalling unjust relationships existing in our world. This plea for justice is clearly heard first in the Old Testament prophets, then again in the last of the prophets—John the Baptist—and finally Jesus himself." Cardinal Walter Kasper, *Mercy: The Essence of the Gospel and the Key to Christian Life*, trans. William Madges (Mahwah, NJ: Paulist Press, 2013), 17.

3. Ibid., 88.

4. Ibid., 21.

5. Ibid., 43.

6. For a handy resource regarding Catholic social teaching on an option for the poor, see "Catholic Social Teaching on Poverty, an Option for the Poor, and the Common Good," available from the United States Conference of Catholic Bishops, which may be accessed at: http://www.usccb.org/about/domestic-social-development/resources/upload/poverty-common-good-CST.pdf. For an excellent reflection on contemporary implications of an option for the poor, see Paul Farmer and Gustavo Gutierrez, *In the Company of the Poor: Conversations with Dr. Paul Farmer and Fr. Gustavo Gutierrez*, ed. Michael Griffin and Jennie Weiss Block (Maryknoll, NY: Orbis, 2013).

7. The work of mercy, to bury the dead, comes from the Book of Tobit.

8. Kasper, *Mercy*, 143.

9. Ibid., 143–44.

10. Christine D. Pohl, *Making Room: Recovering Hospitality as a Christian Tradition* (Grand Rapids, MI: William B. Eerdmans, 1999), 16.

11. Ibid., 13.

12. Patricia and Dan have been married twenty-five years.

13. In this reflection, we do not hear Bob claiming he can save himself (a Pelagian argument that is heretical). In other words, he is not claiming to save himself through his works. Rather, Bob and Jeanne feel compelled by faith to extend mercy to this particular man, and in doing so, understand themselves to be answering a call from God. The God who saves is asking them to be faithful and hospitable even when it is difficult, and they believe there is redemption in answering that call.

14. Mark and Joanne are in full support of their son's legal marriage to his same-sex partner. Joanne told us that she and Mark are flattered that Charlie and his husband have "said a number of times that they are modeling their marriage on ours, that [our marriage] is encouraging to them." Joanne and Mark feel some vulnerability in their work in the Catholic church because of their openness regarding their support of same-sex marriage, but are committed to "living authentically" even at the risk of their jobs. Joanne said, "Having a gay child has really made us look at our faith. And ask questions. And come to know that our lived reality—our experience—is Godly. And so is our child! And, I'm sorry, but the bishops don't speak for me regarding their approach to homosexuality." In one of our focus groups, a father told us that two of his eight adult daughters came out as lesbian in recent years. He described it as "a challenge" for their family and said, "I think our faith really pulled us through in that. We just concluded that love is unconditional and I guess we, following Pope Francis, [say,]'Who are we to judge?' We just go with the flow, and they are the most loving kids."

15. Julie Hanlon Rubio, *Family Ethics: Practices for Christians* (Washington, DC: Georgetown University Press, 2010), 199.

16. Ibid., 201.

17. Ibid.

Chapter 5   pages 85–100

1. Justice, prudence, courage and temperance are classically seen as the cardinal virtues, the central virtues on which all others build.

2. C. S. Lewis, *The Four Loves* (New York: Harcourt Brace, 1960), 121.

3. Brené Brown, *Daring Greatly: How the Courage to Be Vulnerable Transforms the Way We Live, Love, Parent, and Lead* (New York: Gotham, 2012), 12.

4. Ibid., 34.

5. Ibid.

6. C. S. Lewis, *The Four Loves*, 122.

7. We do not mean to downplay the difficulty caused by finances which are known to be a serious challenge to marital success. See, for instance, the work

of Sonya Britt, a Kansas State University researcher, who notes that couples that argued about money early in their relationships—regardless of their income, debt, or net worth—were at a greater risk for divorce. "Arguments about money [are] by far the top predictor of divorce," she said. "It's not children, sex, in-laws or anything else. It's money—for both men and women" (Divorce Study: Financial Arguments Early in Relationship May Predict Divorce, July 12, 2013, http://www.huffingtonpost.com/2013/07/12/divorce-study_n_3587811 .html). What our couples evidenced was an ability to stand together and support one another when financial difficulties beset them.

    8. Robert Ellsberg, *The Saints' Guide to Happiness: Everyday Wisdom from the Lives and Lore of the Saints* (New York: North Point, 2003), 104.

    9. Ibid., 104.

    10. Ibid., 122.

    11. Ibid., 126.

    12. Ibid., 135.

    13. Richard R. Gaillardetz, *A Daring Promise: A Spirituality of Christian Marriage* (Liguori, MO: Liguori/Triumph, 2007), 23.

    14. Ibid., 24.

    15. Ellsberg, *Saints' Guide to Happiness*, 111.

    16. We share in this chapter several stories of couples who lost children. We heard even more stories than we relay here, and it was clear that the loss of a child was a profound stressor for these couples. One might assume they "beat the odds" by not ending up divorced, but we note research that suggests that more marriages survive the death of a child than may widely be assumed: "Despite a widespread belief that the death of a child and the divorce of the parents are virtual cause and effect, this survey strongly suggests this to be a myth, confirming the results of the 1999 survey of The Compassionate Friends, as well as another study released the same year by two University of Montana professors." (From the report "When a Child Dies: A Survey of Bereaved Parents" http:// www.compassionatefriends.org/pdf/When_a_Child_Dies-2006_Final.pdf). We relay these stories, then, not in an effort to uncover how these couples beat the odds, but from the perspective of understanding how they effectively dealt with what is inarguably a tremendous experience of suffering.

    17. Ellsberg, *Saints' Guide to Happiness*, 135–6.

    18. An additional 26 percent indicated a sense of humor was somewhat important for a total of 97 percent; an additional 17 percent indicated patience was somewhat important for a total of 97 percent; and an additional 28 percent indicated hope was somewhat important, for a total of 95 percent of couples surveyed attesting to the importance of these virtues when they navigate struggles or suffering.

    19. When asked about times of stress or struggle, 58 percent said support from their family was extremely important, and 32 percent said it was somewhat

important; 43 percent said support from their friends was extremely important, and 47 percent said it was somewhat important; 39 percent said support from their church community was extremely important, and 46 percent said it was somewhat important.

20. Stanley Hauerwas, *God, Medicine, and Suffering* (Grand Rapids, MI: William B. Eerdmans, 1994), xi.

21. Ibid., 151.

Chapter 6 pages 101–126

1. James Keenan, "Virtue Ethics and Sexual Ethics," *Louvain Studies* 30, no. 3 (Fall 2005): 195.

2. Ibid., 192.

3. Or, in another approved version of vows for a Catholic liturgy, "until death do us part."

4. Margaret Farley, *Personal Commitments: Beginning, Keeping, Changing*, 2nd ed. (Maryknoll, NY: Orbis, 2013), 21.

5. Ibid.

6. This "new relation" is often explicitly stated by the one presiding: "I now pronounce you husband and wife."

7. Farley, *Personal Commitments*, 22.

8. Ibid., 57.

9. Ibid., 23.

10. Michael Lawler, "Marriage in the Bible" in *Perspectives on Marriage: A Reader*, 2nd ed., ed. Kieran Scott and Michael Warren (New York: Oxford University Press, 2001), 12.

11. Ibid., 16.

12. Ibid., 18–19.

13. Farley, *Personal Commitments*, 152.

14. Lawler, "Marriage in the Bible," 19.

15. Ibid. Italics ours.

16. Ibid., 20.

17. In our written surveys, only 5 percent of respondents claimed that communication styles were *never* a source of conflict in their marriage. A full 60 percent of couples *sometimes* experience communication styles as a source of conflict, while 26 percent *often* do. Moreover, 6 percent of respondents report that communication styles *very often* cause conflict in their marriage.

18. The Raders told a story about ongoing tension in their marriage over Laura's habit of collecting boxes and piling them in the basement. In short, it drove Jeff "crazy." One day while Laura was out, Jeff tried to get to the water heater in the basement, which was blocked by piles and piles of collected boxes. He hit his breaking point. When Laura came home, she saw smoke coming

from the backyard. She went back to find Jeff throwing boxes in a bonfire. Laura said, "I couldn't even be mad. I thought it was so funny. Did we stoop to this level? It's pretty juvenile actually. So I go up to him and say, 'What are you doing?' And he goes—he could hardly keep from laughing either and he goes—'Burning your boxes!'" Laura said, "We kind of wanted to still be mad at each other but" they could "hardly keep from laughing. Finally, he goes, 'Well, I didn't burn *all* of them!'"

19. Years ago, in a local parish, during an informational session for parents about reconciliation, the pastor said something like: "The sacrament of reconciliation is fundamentally a celebration of the fact that there is nothing you can do—I mean, *nothing* you can do—that would keep God from loving you." We were reminded of this profound statement when Angie and Jerry Smith were talking about the struggles of parenting children, even into adulthood, and the need for parents to trust and allow their adult children to make mistakes but for the parents to remain faithful to their children. Through fidelity and forgiveness in family life, Jerry and Angie better understand the abundant mercy of God. Angie said, "That's where I see God's love. That's where I see that no matter what [our children] do, it's always forgivable. I think, *wow, I can't imagine what one of my kids would do or what Jerry would do that I couldn't forgive . . . or I couldn't love them through it even if they weren't contrite about it or something.* And I think, *That's how much God loves and cherishes—well, more!—me and each one of them.*

20. Paul Wadell, *Becoming Friends: Worship, Justice, and the Practice of Christian Friendship* (Grand Rapids, MI: Brazos, 2002), 166–167.

21. Ibid., 167.

22. Paul Wadell writes: "Prayer is important for cultivating the gracious imagination necessary for forgiveness because through prayer we remember, for example, that we too have often stood in need of forgiveness from our friends and relied on them to offer it. . . . Moreover, prayer is indispensable for forgiveness because it reminds us, first, that all forgiveness, even our most feeble efforts, is rooted in the forgiveness of God. None of us forgives out of his [sic] own resources of mercy; rather, our forgiveness always shares in and flows from the forgiveness and mercy of God." Ibid., 178.

23. Rebecca Konynkyk DeYoung, *Glittering Vices: A New Look at the Seven Deadly Sins and Their Remedies* (Grand Rapids, MI: Brazos, 2009), 86–87.

24. Ibid., 86.

25. Farley, *Personal Commitments*, 39.

26. Ibid.

27. Ibid., 60.

28. Ibid., 62.

29. Ibid.

30. Psychologist Judith Wallerstein explains that when couples embark on a romantic love relationship, "They engage in a full-blown idealization of the

other—an idealization rooted in the wishes and hopes of childhood. The new love is larger than life, endowed with the ability to deliver whatever one's heart desires. Generations of parents have learned that it is impossible to introduce a different perspective at the height of a new romance because the lovers have blocked our reality." Judith Wallerstein and Sandra Blakeslee, *The Good Marriage: How and Why Love Lasts* (New York: Warner, 1995), 47.

31. Farley, *Personal Commitments*, 62–63.

32. Ibid., 63.

33. Ibid., 64.

34. Ibid., 63.

35. Ibid., 69.

36. Ibid., 71.

37. Ibid., 73.

38. Wallerstein, *The Good Marriage*, 324.

39. Ibid.

40. Farley, *Personal Commitments*, 59.

41. This particular focus group consisted of four couples who respectively have been married forty-two, forty-eight, fifty-five, and fifty-seven years.

42. Without making judgments or exhibiting self-righteousness, a great many couples in our study expressed sadness about the marriages around them that have ended in divorce. In the words of one woman, divorce of those "most beloved" to us—our parents, our siblings, our friends, those in our church communities—remind us of "the fragility of love" and can inspire us to be more fully attentive to our own relationships. We want to note that there are a handful of participants in our study who have experienced divorce themselves and are now remarried happily and faithfully. We also wish to note that, by upholding fidelity as an ideal, we do not wish to imply that spouses should stay in a relationship that is abusive or dehumanizing. For a marriage to live up to its potential, both partners must be faithfully committed to the covenant relationship that includes actively seeking the good of his or her spouse. Fidelity is meant to foster life-giving relationship.

Conclusion   pages 127–137

1. We are encouraged by the fact that the magisterium made efforts to hear the experiences of married faithful in preparation for the 2014 Extraordinary Synod on the Family. That said, those efforts seemed inconsistent, with some bishops reportedly seeking input only from ordained clergy in their dioceses. In a commentary on the preparatory document for the synod that resulted from those efforts, Thomas Reese, SJ, called it "boring and joyless." ("Synod Paper is Boring and Joyless," *National Catholic Reporter*, June 27, 2014, http://ncronline .org/blogs/faith-and-justice/synod-working-paper-boring-and-joyless). How sad.

And how unlike the joy and hope we experienced when listening to married couples tell us about their faith and lives.

2. To be fair, outside of this particular question, sometimes couples referred to magisterial teaching in a more positive light, praising the church's high regard for the sanctity of life, for example, or its promotion of the goodness of sexuality in a culture that trivializes it. But couples did not refer to specific documents when doing so.

Appendix   pages 138–147

1. Fifteen of the parishes were located in the geographically expansive diocese, and five were located in the major urban/suburban area.

2. This survey item read, "The researchers are interested in interviewing couples whose marriages are identified by others as being especially vibrant and who serve as models of what holiness can look like in everyday life. Please name one or more couples in your parish community who you would describe in this way."

3. Paper distribution was chosen for several reasons, including greater confidence for participants that responses were anonymous and greater distribution ease for the parish staff member (who may not have email addresses for all parishioners).

4. Four parishes, or 20 percent of the sample, requested some or all of the surveys in Spanish.

5. That is, 84 percent of all couples invited to participate returned at least one survey.

6. The survey item asking about religious affiliation did provide other options, including Buddhist, Hindu, Jewish, Muslim, and atheist/agnostic, but these were not selected by any respondents.

7. *U.S. Religious Landscape Survey,* "Chapter Three: Religious Affiliation and Demographic Groups," Pew Research Center, Washington, DC, 2008. http://religions.pewforum.org/pdf/report-religious-landscape-study-chapter-3.pdf.

8. Ibid., 9.

9. Ibid., 21.

10. Ibid., 25.

11. 58.8 percent of those without a high school diploma had experienced divorce as compared to 29.8 percent of those with a bachelor's degree or higher. *Marriage and Divorce Patterns by Gender, Race and Educational Attainment,* Bureau of Labor and Statistics, October 2013. http://www.bls.gov/opub/mlr/2013/article/marriage-and-divorce-patterns-by-gender-race-and-educational-attainment.htm.

12. Ibid., 49.1 percent for those with no college experience and 48.5 percent for those with some college experience, again as compared to 29.8 percent for those who completed at least a bachelor's degree.

13. M. D. Bramlett and W. D. Mosher, *Cohabitation, Marriage, Divorce, and Remarriage in the United States,* National Center for Health Statistics, *Vital Health Stat* 23 (2002). http://www.cdc.gov/nchs/data/series/sr_23/sr23_022.pdf.

Bibliography

Anderson, Herbert, Edward Foley, Bonnie Miller-McLemore and Robert Schreiter, eds. *Mutuality Matters: Family, Faith, and Just Love*. Lanham, MD: Rowman & Littlefield, 2004.

Belkin, Lisa. "When Mom and Dad Share It All." *New York Times Magazine* (June 15, 2008). http://www.nytimes.com.

Bourg, Florence Caffrey. *Where Two or Three Are Gathered: Christian Families as Domestic Churches*. Notre Dame: University of Notre Dame, 2004.

Brown, Brené. *Daring Greatly: How the Courage to Be Vulnerable Transforms the Way We Live, Love, Parent, and Lead*. New York: Gotham, 2012.

Cahill, Lisa Sowle. *Family: A Christian Social Perspective*. Minneapolis: Fortress, 2000.

Congregation for the Doctrine of the Faith. *Letter to the Bishops of the Catholic Church on the Collaboration of Men and Women in the Church and in the World*. http://www.vatican.va.

DeYoung, Rebecca Konyndyk. *Glittering Vices: A New Look at the Seven Deadly Sins and Their Remedies*. Grand Rapids, MI: Brazos, 2009.

Ellison, Marvin M. "Reimagining Good Sex: The Eroticizing of Mutual Respect and Pleasure." In *Sexuality and the Sacred: Sources for Theological Reflection*, 2nd ed., edited by Marvin M. Ellison and Kelly Brown Douglas, 245–261. Louisville, KY: Westminster John Knox, 2010.

Ellsberg, Robert. *The Saints' Guide to Happiness: Everyday Wisdom from the Lives and Lore of the Saints*. New York: North Point, 2003.

Farley, Margaret. *Personal Commitments: Beginning, Keeping, Changing*, revised edition. Maryknoll, NY: Orbis, 2013.

Feiler, Bruce. *The Secrets of Happy Families: Improve Your Mornings, Rethink Family Dinner, Fight Smarter, Go Out and Play, and Much More*. New York: William Morrow, 2013.

Gaillardetz, Richard R. *A Daring Promise: A Spirituality of Christian Marriage*. 2nd ed. Liguori, MO: Liguori/Triumph, 2007.

Gallagher, Maureen. "Family as Sacrament." In *The Changing Family: Views from Theology and the Social Sciences in Light of the Apostolic* Exhortation Familiaris Consortio, edited by Stanley L. Saxton, Patricia Voydanoff, and Angela Ann Zukowski, 5–13. Chicago: Loyola University Press, 1984.

Hauerwas, Stanley. *God, Medicine, and Suffering*. Grand Rapids, MI: William B. Eerdmans, 1994.

Himes, Michael J. "Finding God in All Things: A Sacramental Worldview and Its Effects." In *Becoming Beholders: Cultivating Sacramental Imagination and Actions in College Classrooms*, edited by Karen E. Eifler and Thomas M. Landy, 3–17. Collegeville, MN: Liturgical Press, 2014.

John Paul II. *Sollicitudo Rei Socialis* (On Social Concern). Vatican Web site, December 30, 1987. http://www.vatican.va.

Julian of Norwich. *Meditations with Julian of Norwich*. Edited by Brendan Doyle. Santa Fe, NM: Bear & Company, Inc., 1983.

Jung, L. Shannon. *Sharing Food: Christian Practices for Enjoyment*. Minneapolis: Fortress, 2006.

Kasper, Cardinal Walter. *Mercy: The Essence of the Gospel and the Key to Christian Life*. Translated by William Madges. Mahwah, NJ: Paulist Press, 2013.

Keenan, James. "Virtue Ethics and Sexual Ethics." *Louvain Studies* 30, no. 2 (Fall 2005), 180–196.

Kimmel, Michael. *Guyland: The Perilous World Where Boys Become Men*. New York: Harper, 2008.

Lawler, Michael. "Marriage in the Bible." In *Perspectives on Marriage: A Reader*, 2nd ed., edited by Kieran Scott and Michael Warren, 7–21. New York: Oxford University Press, 2001.

Lewis, C. S. *The Four Loves*. New York: Harcourt Brace, 1960.

McBrien, Richard P. *Catholicism*. Minneapolis: Winston, 1980.

McFague, Sallie. *Models of God: Theology for an Ecological, Nuclear Age*. Philadelphia: Fortress, 1987.

National Marriage Project. *When Baby Makes Three: How Parenthood Makes Life Meaningful and How Marriage Makes Parenting Bearable*, edited by W. Bradford Wilcox and Elizabeth Marquardt. Charlottesville, VA: National Marriage Project and the Institute for American Values, 2011.

———. *When Marriage Disappears: The New Middle America*, edited by W. Bradford Wilcox and Elizabeth Marquardt. Charlottesville, VA: National Marriage Project and the Institute for American Values, 2010.

Paul VI, Pope. *Humanae Vitae* (Human Life). Vatican Website, July 26, 1968. http://www.vatican.va.

———. *Lumen Gentium* (Dogmatic Constitution on the Church), Vatican website, November 21, 1964. http://www.vatican.va.

Pohl, Christine D. *Making Room: Recovering Hospitality as a Christian Tradition*. Grand Rapids, MI: William B. Eerdmans, 1999.

Rubio, Julie Hanlon. *A Christian Theology of Marriage and Family*. Mahwah, NJ: Paulist Press, 2003.

———. *Family Ethics: Practices for Christians*. Washington, DC: Georgetown University Press, 2010.

Ross, Susan A. *Extravagant Affections: A Feminist Sacramental Theology*. New York: Continuum, 1998.

Saiving, Valerie. "The Human Situation: A Feminine View." In *Womanspirit Rising: A Feminist Reader in Religion*, edited by Carol P. Christ and Judith Plaskow, 25–42. New York: Harper & Row, 1979.

Scott, Kieran, and Michael Warren, eds. *Perspectives on Marriage: A Reader*, 2nd ed. Oxford: Oxford University Press, 2001.

Steiner-Adair, Catherine, and Teresa H. Barker. *The Big Disconnect: Protecting Childhood and Family Relationships in the Digital Age*. New York: HarperCollins, 2013.

Traina, Cristina L. H. "Under Pressure: Sexual Discipleship in the Real World." In *Sexuality and the U.S. Catholic Church: Crisis and Renewal*, edited by Lisa Sowle Cahill, John Garvey, and Thomas Frank Kennedy, 68–93. New York: Crossroad, 2006.

United States Conference of Catholic Bishops. *Marriage: Life and Love in the Divine Plan*. Washington, DC: USCCB, 2009.